The Story of Joseph and the Family of Jacob

Ronald S. Wallace

WILLIAM B. EERDMANS PUBLISHING COMPANY
GRAND RAPIDS, MICHIGAN

RUTHERFORD HOUSE
EDINBURGH, U.K.

Published jointly 2001
in the United States of America by
Wm. B. Eerdmans Publishing Co.
255 Jefferson Ave. S.E., Grand Rapids, Michigan 49503
www.eerdmans.com
and in the U.K. by
Rutherford House
17 Claremont Park
Edinburgh EH6 7PJ

Printed in the United States of America

06 05 04 03 02 01   7 6 5 4 3 2 1

Library of Congress Cataloging-in-Publication Data

Wallace, Ronald S.
The story of Joseph and the family of Jacob / Ronald S. Wallace
p.   cm.
ISBN 0-8028-4808-7 (pbk.: alk. paper)
1. Joseph (Son of Jacob) 2. Patriarchs (Bible) — Biography. 3. Bible. O.T. Genesis — Biography. 4. Bible. O.T. Genesis XXXVII-L — Criticism, interpretation, etc. I. Title

BS580.J6 W35 2001
222′.1107 — dc21

00-045614

British Library Cataloguing-in-Publication Data

A catalogue record for this book
is available from the British Library

Rutherford House ISBN 0-946068-81-X

to my late sister
Mary

Contents

Contents

Foreword

It is over twenty years since I published my expository studies, first on *Abraham,* and then on *Isaac and Jacob.* Though these were well received I did not feel I could confidently issue what I had then written on the Joseph stories. I have since then been able to profit in my understanding of the whole Bible by a deepening appreciation of the place taken in the Old Testament by the prophetic development of salvation history as it moves towards Christ. I have found this growing insight especially helpful in the exposition I now feel able to offer of these closing chapters of the Book of Genesis.

I hope this book will be of use not only to the individual Bible student, but also in group discussion. I have written and arranged the text so as to provoke discussion questions as it is read through. The story itself is richly provocative of fresh meaning. The text used is that of the New Revised Standard Version.

I am again greatly in debt to my brother-in-law, the Rev. Dr. Robert B. W. Walker, for his skill in deciphering my hasty writing and in feeding and working his computer so as to produce a perfect typescript. For careful and helpful proofreading I am grateful to my sister-in-law, Dr. Elizabeth Torrance. It was both a help and a pleasure when the Rev. David Searle of Rutherford House, who has always greatly encouraged me to keep on writing, offered to sponsor a U.K. edition of the book. I had hoped that my sister Mary, who died shortly before its publication, would find pleasure in receiving the book, which I have dedicated to her memory. I have always been grateful for her.

CHAPTER 1

The Family of Jacob (1)

Genesis 37:1-11

37 Jacob settled in the land where his father had lived as an alien, the land of Canaan. ²This is the story of the family of Jacob.

Joseph, being seventeen years old, was shepherding the flock with his brothers; he was a helper to the sons of Bilhah and Zilpah, his father's wives; and Joseph brought a bad report of them to his father. ³Now Israel loved Joseph more than any other of his children, because he was the son of his old age; and he had made him a long robe with sleeves. ⁴But when his brothers saw that their father loved him more than all his brothers, they hated him, and could not speak peaceably to him.

⁵Once Joseph had a dream, and when he told it to his brothers, they hated him even more. ⁶He said to them, "Listen to this dream that I dreamed. ⁷There we were, binding sheaves in the field. Suddenly my sheaf rose and stood upright; then your sheaves gathered around it, and bowed down to my sheaf." ⁸His brothers said to him, "Are you indeed to reign over us? Are you indeed to have dominion over us?" So they hated him even more because of his dreams and his words.

⁹He had another dream, and told it to his brothers, saying, "Look, I have had another dream: the sun, the moon, and eleven stars were bowing down to me." ¹⁰But when he told it to his father and to his

brothers, his father rebuked him, and said to him, "What kind of dream is this that you have had? Shall we indeed come, I and your mother and your brothers, and bow to the ground before you?" [11]So his brothers were jealous of him, but his father kept the matter in mind.

A House Divided Against Itself

Jacob, as we read of him at this point in his career, has already lost his grip over his family to an extent and in a way he would never in his early days have imagined possible. Gone almost completely was his fervor for the faith which in his early days had won God's forgiveness even for his misplaced zeal, and had earned him also the new name Israel ("Prince with God"). He seems to have allowed himself to drift and is no longer able to lead or even to speak confidently on what most matters even with his own family.

Of course had he maintained with them a common faith and sense of purpose, and exercised a strong, wise, and fatherly rule, it would have been extremely difficult to overcome their natural divisions and to hold them all together with a sense of belonging with love and respect for each other. The sons of Leah — six of them, the majority — felt themselves superior and kept to themselves in family affairs because they were older. They would tend naturally to distance themselves from Joseph because Leah their mother had felt she suffered so much in her bitter rivalry with Rachel, Joseph's dead mother. They had tended to go each his own way. We read of Simeon and Levi's deceit and brutality (Gen. 34:25ff.), of Reuben's incest (Gen. 35:22), and of Judah's fickleness and lechery (Gen. 38). Moreover, Jacob himself had kept alive in their minds the memory of his preference for Rachel by making Joseph his favorite, dressing him in an exclusive *"long robe with sleeves"* (Gen. 37:3). The story indicates that the younger group of brothers, Dan, Naphtali, Gad, and Asher — the sons of Bilhah and Zilpah (37:2) — had followed largely in the footsteps of their older brothers. They were close to each other in age, though older than Joseph. But it was with them that Joseph had had to learn to mix and play (v. 2). Though they may have felt themselves at times pushed aside by the sons of Leah, they were nevertheless at one with them in their dislike of Jacob's obviously favorite son.

Joseph, on his part, found himself different from the whole family in tastes, values, aims, and beliefs. He did not fit the accepted pattern, and the talk and behavior of his forced companions caused him such revulsion that on one fatal occasion he poured out his misery and confessed his utter loneliness and deep concern to his father. The brothers had continually found him "difficult," had never been able to fit him into their plans or their common activities. They never forgot that he had "told" on them, and they determined to pay him back.

What made Joseph so radically different from his brothers comes to full light in his rejection of Potiphar's wife: "How can I do this great wickedness and sin against God?" (39:9). The division within the family involved much deeper issues than who belonged to which mother, or who had a long-sleeved coat and who had none. We can understand it fully only by realizing that the brothers at this time were, as a body, deliberately adopting aims and values of their own, in reaction to the family tradition. Only Joseph, apart and alone, had listened and responded to the same call that had isolated Abraham, Isaac, and Jacob from their "world," the call that had made them men of God and different. In Joseph, the brothers faced a new and vital embodiment of the view of God and life they had already excluded from their own pattern and way of things. They hated him the more because they clearly recognized it in him. Each in his turn had crushed it from within himself. Joseph to them was what they had decided not to be.

The Word of God

It is within this sad and bitter family setting that Joseph has his two dreams. We need not be suspicious of the narrative's factuality because dreams figure so largely within it. Dreams, in these far-off days, were a means by which superstitious people believed they received uncanny communications from the other world about their future. Pagan deities were supposed to use dreams to make known their whims and to give hints of their next moves in the game of life. People became afraid when their dreams were ominous, happy when their dreams were propitious. They believed in dreams and they could become controlled by them. In such a world, then, why should God, too, not also communicate with his people through the media they accepted? Later on, of course, after the children of Israel had lived longer under God's education, the great prophets found the Word of God coming to them in ways that marked their sources of inspiration as clearly different from those of their pagan neighbors. But at this stage in the pilgrimage these later standards were not possible. God took his people as they were, and sometimes used the usual channels to intimate his will and convey his Word about things to come.

God gave his Word to the family of Jacob through two dreams, the one reinforcing the other; and he chose Joseph to be the prophet who would receive them. The boy immediately recognized their significance, their compelling authority and power. He knew that most dreams, produced by causes naturally explainable, need not be taken seriously, but he believed these two were shaped by God. They came in a special way with unique force, burning themselves into his memory. "Joseph had often dreamed in a common manner," comments

Calvin, "but here Moses shows that a dream was now divinely sent which might have the force of an oracle." Joseph felt that it was a genuine message from God to his family, justifying the stand he had been called to take about the family tradition. He did not dare to hide the Word that God had given him. No doubt he shrank from telling it, for he knew his family might hate him for what he would say. He struggled, no doubt, against the word he had to speak. Like the prophet Jeremiah, he held himself in as long as he could, in a vain effort to keep back what he was terrified to utter (Jer. 20:9; 6:11). Yet he may have felt that by a sheer miracle of grace, God might incline them to listen to what he had to say. Like Jeremiah, too, eventually he had to blurt out the truth. It came awkwardly but authoritatively. *"Hear this dream,"* he announced, and, as if delivering a solemn oracle from God, he told about how his sheaf would one day stand upright in the field and his brothers' sheaves would come round and bow down, and he followed it with the next dream — even more mysterious and offensive: *"Behold, I have dreamed another dream: and behold, the sun, the moon, and eleven stars were bowing down to me"* (v. 9, RSV).

To the young prophet uttering his oracle, it was the father's reaction that was unexpected and shattering. We are told that the dreams' content registered powerfully with the old man, for he *"kept the saying in mind"* (v. 11). But what he said on the spot before the family expressed something of the exasperation felt by everyone else present. He interpreted the dreams in a literal way that tended to make Joseph all the more ridiculous. *"What is this dream that you have dreamed? Shall I and your mother and your brothers indeed come to bow ourselves to the ground before you?"* (v. 10, RSV). We can perhaps understand Jacob's motives. He wanted peace and unity. He had not realized till that moment how tense the situation was in his home. He may have felt that he had gone too far in encouraging this youngster over against his brothers, and in dressing him in that coat! He was trying to redress the balance and appear impartial.

Our narrator does not describe Joseph's feelings. His art is always to delineate carefully the tense and dramatic situation and to pause so that we can simply let the whole story register. We are meant to feel within ourselves what Joseph felt at this most acute moment in all his sufferings so far. The only friend he thought he had in the world — the *one* support — had failed him, just when he had needed him most! Jeremiah was in a similar situation early in his ministry. His ministry in the countryside and in Jerusalem had culminated in his dramatic attack on the worship in the temple at Jerusalem (Jer. 7). No doubt he had said many things in public that hurt his own family in the village of Anathoth, a family that was proud of its priestly descent. The Word that came to him said that even they were plotting his destruction: "Even your brothers and the house of your father, even they have dealt treacherously with you; they are in full cry after you; believe them not though they speak fair words to you" (Jer. 12:6). Isolated by the Word of God from everyone he had loved, he expressed himself in personal utterances of almost unsurpassed pathos. "Woe is me, my mother, that you bore me, a man of strife and contention to the whole land!" (Jer. 15:10, 15-18).

When Jesus said, "I have come to set a man against his father" (Matt. 10:35), he may have been thinking back to Jeremiah and even to Joseph. He too knew how obedience to the Word of God sometimes isolated a man from his family (John 7:5). Abraham must have experienced something of it when he was called to leave kindred in Haran to go to the promised land. Here is Joseph — and he is only seventeen years old!

When we make our judgment on Joseph as a person we must make allowance for the unusual prophetic responsibility he bore under the Word of God so early in his life. Many preachers and expositors too easily find ground for calling him a "tale-bearer." Some picture him as actively trying to steal his father's favor at the expense of his brothers. Some think that he needlessly provoked his brothers by telling the dreams he should have kept to himself. Some blame him for what they feel is an egocentric emphasis in the telling: "*my sheaf . . . stood upright . . . your sheaves . . . bowed down to my sheaf*" (v. 7). In making up our minds about this boy, then, we have to remember the words of Jesus: "You will know them by their fruits" (Matt. 7:16). We have to remember also his warning that as the seed of the kingdom grows in the human heart, there may take place for a time only a gradual and undramatic development: "First the blade, then the ear, then the full grain in the ear" (Mark 4:28). We must not despise the unimpressive blade just because we do not yet see the ear! A biographer of St. Francis de Sales points out that in a developing spiritual life what can be taken as evidence of genuine God-centered sanctity can also be mistaken as evidence of its caricature — self-centered priggishness. It is "not always easy to distinguish the one from the other in saints' lives," he remarks — though in the genuine saint we will be ultimately left in no doubt. We must therefore interpret this part of the story by giving Joseph the benefit of the doubt. Instead of accusing him of "telling tales," we have to remember that there is "a time to keep silence and a time to speak" (Eccles. 3:7), and that indeed under certain circumstances it can be wrong not to speak (cf. Ps. 105:19).

"They Hated Him Even More"

The Word of God never leaves us neutral. It forces us to decide for or against what it demands or promises. Once it enters and takes root in the mind and heart, the whole person begins to be reoriented and moved towards true love and goodness. Those who resist the truth and its challenge, however, find themselves in practice forced more and more to resist the goodness they reject. In the Gospel of John the opposition of those who reject Jesus is at first a mere questioning, but soon becomes an intent to kill him. It finds expression in an increasingly virulent campaign of words meant to destroy his influence. Eventually a plot has to be made and finally they crucify him.

"He who is not with me," said Jesus, "is against me. He who gathers not with me scatters" (Matt. 12:30). The brothers of Joseph are thus gradually drawn into a more and more determined opposition. The brothers understood the dreams well — as an immediate challenge to their entrenched opposition to Joseph! What he had dreamed was an urgent call to think again about the issues, and to change their attitude willingly before they were forced to submission. The dreams were sent to help them, if they would, to become more humble, before they were finally humiliated.

The message of the dreams was intended for them as a Word of God, vindicating young Joseph and everything he stood for in their family tradition. It was a warning that their opposition must finally lead them nowhere. They must now willingly turn back to the ways they had forsaken, look at the truth they were tempted to evade and hate, and allow themselves to be drawn back into it. Here was God acting in his grace and appealing through their young brother, calling on them to halt and change. Here was the way to a true family unity that could there and then have been restored. Here was the most direct road to the fulfillment of God's purpose for their family. They decided to resist. They quenched the spirit in themselves and they determined to quench it in their young brother. Now the issue is clearer. No longer do they hate him because of his long-sleeved coat or his father's favoritism; they hate him because they have heard the truth about God, and themselves, from his lips — and they know it. Now *they hated him even more because of his dreams and his words*" (v. 8).

For a penetrating discussion of the brothers' final reaction to the two dreams we turn to Calvin's commentary on the passage. Calvin is writing from his lifelong experience as a preacher who often himself found some of his hearers rejecting the Word of God. "It often happens," he writes, "that they who are ill-disposed quickly perceive what *is* the will of God, but because they feel no reverence they despise it." Calvin believed that in the incident before us the brothers, as they listened, clearly understood the will of God. They knew clearly that they were being threatened on account of it. But they decided to become more set in their resistance. "With or against their will, they are compelled to feel there is something authentic in the dream. Yet a blind ferocity impels them to . . . resistance against God."

CHAPTER 2

The Family of Jacob (2)

Genesis 37:12-36

37 ¹²Now the brothers went to pasture their father's flock near Shechem. ¹³And Israel said to Joseph, "Are not your brothers pasturing the flock at Shechem? Come, I will send you to them." He answered, "Here I am." ¹⁴So he said to him, "Go now, see if it is well with your brothers and with the flock; and bring word back to me." So he sent him from the valley of Hebron.

He came to Shechem, ¹⁵and a man found him wandering in the fields; the man asked him, "What are you seeking?" ¹⁶"I am seeking my brothers," he said, "tell me, please, where they are pasturing the flock." ¹⁷The man said, "They have gone away; for I heard them say, 'Let us go to Dothan.'" So Joseph went after his brothers, and found them at Dothan. ¹⁸They saw him from a distance, and before he came near to them, they conspired to kill him. ¹⁹They said to one another, "Here comes this dreamer. ²⁰Come now, let us kill him and throw him into one of the pits; then we shall say that a wild animal has devoured him, and we shall see what will become of his dreams." ²¹But when Reuben heard it, he delivered him out of their hands, saying, "Let us not take his life." ²²Reuben said to them, "Shed no blood; throw him into this pit here in the wilderness, but lay no hand on him" — that he might rescue him out of their hand and restore him to his father. ²³So when

Joseph came to his brothers, they stripped him of his robe, the long robe with sleeves that he wore; 24and they took him and threw him into a pit. The pit was empty; there was no water in it.

25Then they sat down to eat; and looking up they saw a caravan of Ishmaelites coming from Gilead, their camels carrying gum, balm, and resin, on their way to carry it down to Egypt. 26Then Judah said to his brothers, "What profit is it if we kill our brother and conceal his blood? 27Come, let us sell him to the Ishmaelites, and not lay our hands on him, for he is our brother, our own flesh." And his brothers agreed. 28When some Midianite traders passed by, they drew Joseph up, lifting him out of the pit, and sold him to the Ishmaelites for twenty pieces of silver. And they took Joseph to Egypt.

29When Reuben returned to the pit and saw that Joseph was not in the pit, he tore his clothes. 30He returned to his brothers, and said, "The boy is gone; and I, where can I turn?" 31Then they took Joseph's robe, slaughtered a goat, and dipped the robe in the blood. 32They had the long robe with the sleeves taken to their father, and they said, "This we have found; see now whether it is your son's robe or not." 33He recognized it and said, "It is my son's robe! A wild animal has devoured him; Joseph is without doubt torn to pieces." 34Then Jacob tore his garments, and put sackcloth on his loins, and mourned for his son many days. 35All his sons and all his daughters rose up to comfort him; but he refused to be comforted, and said, "No, I shall go down to Sheol to my son, mourning." Thus his father bewailed him. 36Meanwhile the Midianites had sold him in Egypt to Potiphar, one of Pharaoh's officials, the captain of the guard.

Joseph's "Here I Am"

"Are not your brothers pasturing the flock at Shechem? Come, I will send you to them." It was a trivial task, for Shechem was fairly near at hand. Joseph was asked merely to take some food for them and to see if all was well. Jacob meant well. He was unaware of the intensity of the hatred stirred up by the telling of the dreams. Joseph, we believe, knew he might be going into real trouble. Since he had told the dreams, every attempt on his part towards even natural and civil communication with his brothers had been stonewalled. He had noticed signs of intensifying hostility. But to him his father's will was God's will. Since the dreams came he was now more than ever God's servant. Possibly the thought occurred to him that such a visit might be an important part of God's plan, too. The dreams had contained God's promise that he would yet win his brothers, that they would bow down to the truth he had been called to serve. Dare he try to hide himself from them, when he was meant by God to seek to win them? Perhaps alone, there in the country, they would give him the chance he had never had with them before: to speak quietly about his hopes, his aims, and his visions. Perhaps they would let him explain the possible meanings of the dreams that he felt he had told too awkwardly.

We ourselves, as we read the story, are meant to be sensitive already to the danger the boy is facing. Up till now, in whatever persecution has come to him through his brothers' anger, he has had the safety of the home and the protection of his father. Now he is to be exposed and defenseless. As well as his loyalty and love we are meant to notice his courage, his faith, and his willingness to be vulnerable as he goes on this mission.

It is deeply significant that in the conversation that took place when Joseph was approached, he replied, *"Here I am"* (v. 13b). Abraham, too, uttered the same words in a similar act of self-surrender when God came to test him on Mount Moriah. God wanted to know

12

how far he was really prepared to go, in trustful obedience, in response to God's Word. In offering Isaac he rose to unprecedented heights of trust and obedience. But it all began when he heard his name called, "Abraham!" and he replied: "Here I am" (Gen. 22:7, 11). As we go through the Bible we will hear the echo of these words again and again, uttered from the lips or spoken in the heart, when others felt themselves called by God. Isaiah, for example, began his prophetic ministry with exactly the same act of self-surrender: "Here am I!" (Isa. 6:8). When we turn to the New Testament we find Jesus calling each of us to make the same self-commitment before we even attempt to follow — "If any will come after me let him deny himself and take up his cross" (Matt. 16:24). His call implies renunciation of our self-will before God, the giving up before God of any claim to self-preservation, to our human safety, to rights or liberty, to comforts and possessions, to friends and reputations — let God now take and do what he will — here we are! "I appeal to you," wrote Paul, ". . . to present your bodies as a living sacrifice, holy and acceptable to God" (Rom. 12:1). The only acceptable sacrifice is a total one, of the whole self, and sometimes we have to make it as Joseph did — in weakness and vulnerability, before enemies against whom we have no defense, before tasks to accomplish in which we have no other conceivable power but God's.

Joseph's concern to share himself with them is shown in the persistence with which he searched till he found them, "*I am seeking my brothers,*" he said everywhere (v. 16). They were not there at Shechem — not, indeed, to be found anywhere in that area! He could easily have gone back to his father then, having literally carried out his orders. But he persisted. He wandered in the fields, hoping for a clue. When he discovered that they had gone as far away as Dothan, he was not daunted. We feel that the narrator is trying to tell us something important, not simply about his activity that day, but also about the whole character and attitude of the boy when he writes, "*So Joseph went after his brothers, and found them*" (v. 17).

13

"This Master of Dreams!"

The next verses of our story (vv. 18-20) show the brothers now admitting to themselves that their chief quarrel is with the Word of God which has been expressed and let loose on them through Joseph's dreams. They hate the dreams as much as they hate the man. *"Here comes this dreamer. Come now, let us kill him and throw him into one of the pits; then we shall say that a wild animal has devoured him, and we shall see what will become of his dreams"* (vv. 19-20). It is Calvin who effectively expresses their sarcasm, translating their nickname for Joseph as *"this master of dreams."*

A modern commentator, Gerhard von Rad, asks us to notice how strongly the element of fear enters their reaction to the dreams of Joseph. He suggests that in the background of these men's thoughts, many of the prevailing superstitions of their day were at work. They believed, for instance, that when a prophet had a dream foretelling the future, and told it to others, then the very act of telling made its prophecy potent; it made the dream come true. Joseph's dreams, once told, were now poised among all the other strange forces they believed could determine the future and make things work out as foretold. In their superstition they believed, too, that if they could now kill the dreamer, the dream itself would collapse and lose its power. How muddled this thinking and how mixed their motives and passions! One thing stands out clearly, though: their hatred of Joseph derives its burning intensity from their hatred of the Word of God. Their anxiety to be rid of him is their anxiety to crush and be rid of the Word of God — if they can. Calvin points out that they should have aimed their blows and insults at God himself. But, he argues, since they did not dare admit even to themselves that they wished to assault God, they wrapped themselves in clouds of ambiguity and lashed out with blows on the one who stood for God — their harmless brother. This fact helps us to understand the demonic intensity of the hatred that possessed them when they saw

14

Joseph even from afar. They transferred what they meant for God to this weak and innocent person.

Von Rad adds his confirmation to this viewpoint. Joseph, he believes, was violently persecuted not simply because he was a prophet, but because, being a prophet, he so closely in himself represented the One he served. The brothers' hate was therefore a rebellion not only against the matter contained in the dreams, but "against the divine power itself, standing behind them, who had given the dreams." Bishop Hall in his comment here reminds us of its virulence: "There is nothing more thankless or dangerous than to stand in the way of a resolute sinner. That which doth correct and oblige the penitent makes the willful mind furious and revengeful." Among all the circumstances in which this crime took place it is worthwhile, even in passing, to note the pervading irrationality of what the brothers thought and planned. How much might have been changed if Joseph had been allowed to come near and speak?

Do we not often go astray because we will not allow Jesus himself to come near to speak his word? Too many of our decisions about life and about God are made with him still a long way off — and they are all wrong! One of the wisest of the prophets asked his generation to let God come close to them simply for talk and sensible discussion. "'Come now, let us argue it out,' says the Lord" (Isa. 1:18). Too often we make our important decisions about people before they are allowed to come near to us, so that we can come to know them, and listen to their reasons and explanations. How distant we prefer to remain so that we can the more easily pass our already determined condemnation on them and on their teachings!

Hatred Comes to Expression

That they really *"hated"* (v. 4) him meant that they had killed him *"before he came near to them"* (v. 18). "When we use the word 'hate,'" writes

Claus Westermann in his recent scholarly study on Joseph, "we usually mean something that is a personal position or attitude. However, in Hebrew, the verb 'to hate' . . . is a deed or the inception of a deed. To practice this kind of hate is like pulling a bowstring taut — it has no purpose unless the arrow is unleashed. . . . Hate as a mere attitude would seem absurd to these people." The New Testament reminds us that though there is a righteous anger which does not involve us in sinning, nevertheless the kind of hatred referred to here is too virulent and dangerous a passion to be given a welcome even for a moment in our minds: "Anyone who hates his brother is a murderer" (1 John 3:15). The calm deliberation with which they thus in their will and imagination executed him *"before he came near"* (vv. 18, 20) reminds us of Esau's determination to kill his brother when his father was dead and the right moment arrived (Gen. 27:41-42).

Their brother was now, by a strange act of providence, isolated, unprotected by his father. There were no possible witnesses around. They no longer needed to fear local censure or any reaction from the rest of the family circle. There was no need in this place for conventional restraint. Led on by the vocal leadership of one or two representing them all, they had in mind and intention stripped him of the garment they hated. They had soaked it in his blood. They had the corpse disposed of where it could never be found. And they were his brothers! "Jacob with his whole Church is subjected to the devil and all his angels to such an extent that it is not strangers, not enemies, not heretics, but sons born from himself, and educated and taught in the Word who kill their innocent brother," says Luther. "They are even worse than Cain." They completely shut down their reason so that nothing could stand in the way of their passion.

We can be thankful for the intervention of Reuben and Judah, who deter the others from giving full vent to what is in their mind when the moment arrives. These two, the oldest, would find themselves more powerfully than the others restrained by their memories of what their father Jacob had passed on to them as a family in the

16

days of his vision and strength. We are bound to regret that they did not make any attempt at intervention earlier. What a difference it would have made if one of them had been willing to stand by Joseph's side for a moment. Yet both had allowed themselves to drift with the family as the rejection of the boy deepened into hatred, and they found themselves bound by silence at the crucial moment of the *"Come, let us kill him"* (v. 20). That God used so effectively their "too little, too late" intervention need not prevent us from exposing their weaknesses in order to learn the lesson they embody. On no occasion, even at the height of the proceedings, do we hear from either of them any decisive protest over what was being attempted. They had an ample store of good intention; yet where a timely voice raised from even one of them at the crucial moment could have altered the whole course of family history, all we hear from them are suggestions about a less bloody and superficially more merciful way of getting rid of the one they have decided to kill. We are reminded of an often quoted adage from John Seeley's *Ecco Homo:* "No heart is pure that is not passionate. No virtue is safe that is not enthusiastic."

"Thus His Father Bewailed Him"

We now return to the fact that Jacob would not have sent Joseph on his mission if he had any suspicion that there was a serious rift between the boy and his brothers. He trusted his sons, and when they came back they had no difficulty in deceiving him. They did not even need to recite in any detail the story they had all agreed to stand by. They showed him the bloodstained robe and said they had found it. Trusting their word, Jacob gave his imagination free rein and convinced himself that his son had been torn to pieces by a wild beast.

Though Jacob had been extraordinarily sharp in business transactions he had never been a good judge of human character, erring always on the side of naïveté. We have to regard this as a fault. We could argue that Jacob was even partly responsible for the crime, for he should not have sent Joseph on his mission. We could argue that because the brothers knew he was so easily deceived they were all the more tempted to deceive him. Nothing, though, can do more damage to the atmosphere of a home than for one member to fail to trust another, for suspicion to prevail, for a habit of overwatchfulness to develop. The possibility of good relationships tends to disappear when detective work begins; love, though never naïve, is always trustful. "Love," said Paul, "bears all things, believes all things, hopes all things" (1 Cor. 13:7). It is not inclined to suspicion. At this stage, it is as well that the old man had no chance of discovering the truth his sons were continually trying to hide from him as they *"rose up to comfort him."* Jacob *"refused to be comforted"* (v. 35). It is worth noting that in their anxiety to comfort the old man they tried hard to seem sincere, when of course they could not be sincere.

We are not meant to forget that this is the family God is going to bless, and make a blessing to all nations. Here are the forefathers of Moses, David, Isaiah, the Psalmists, and all the writers God chose to prepare the way for Christ. They have come down to this and they have well deserved to come down to this. Perhaps as they began to discover how deep, genuine, and inconsolable was their father's grief they began to see what their conscience failed in time to tell them — that all was not well in what they had done. At some time, as the months passed and they all rose up to comfort him, they possibly began to have compunction. Jacob's trust of them at least showed that he loved them in much the same way that he loved his other boy. Of course it was only a weak little stream of trusting love and visible grief. But the small stream constantly flowing over the years — about which we know so little — perhaps began to undermine their resistance to God.

CHAPTER 3

An Introduction to Judah

Genesis 38:1-30

38 It happened at that time that Judah went down from his brothers and settled near a certain Adullamite whose name was Hirah. ² There Judah saw the daughter of a certain Canaanite whose name was Shua; he married her and went in to her. ³ She conceived and bore a son; and he named him Er. ⁴ Again she conceived and bore a son whom she named Onan. ⁵ Yet again she bore a son, and she named him Shelah. She was in Chezib when she bore him. ⁶ Judah took a wife for Er his firstborn; her name was Tamar. ⁷ But Er, Judah's firstborn, was wicked in the sight of the Lord, and the Lord put him to death. ⁸ Then Judah said to Onan, "Go in to your brother's wife and perform the duty of a brother-in-law to her; raise up offspring for your brother." ⁹ But since Onan knew that the offspring would not be his, he spilled his semen on the ground whenever he went in to his brother's wife, so that he would not give offspring to his brother. ¹⁰ What he did was displeasing in the sight of the Lord, and he put him to death also. ¹¹ Then Judah said to his daughter-in-law Tamar, "Remain a widow in your father's house until my son Shelah grows up" — for he feared that he too would die, like his brothers. So Tamar went to live in her father's house.

¹² In course of time the wife of Judah, Shua's daughter, died; when

Judah's time of mourning was over, he went up to Timnah to his sheep-shearers, he and his friend Hirah the Adullamite. 13 When Tamar was told, "Your father-in-law is going up to Timnah to shear his sheep," 14 she put off her widow's garments, put on a veil, wrapped herself up, and sat down at the entrance to Enaim, which is on the road to Timnah. She saw that Shelah was grown up, yet she had not been given to him in marriage. 15 When Judah saw her, he thought her to be a prostitute, for she had covered her face. 16 He went over to her, at the roadside, and said, "Come, let me come into you," for he did not know that she was his daughter-in-law. She said, "What will you give me, that you may come in to me?" 17 He answered, "I will send you a kid from the flock." And she said, "Only if you give me a pledge, until you send it." 18 He said, "What pledge shall I give you?" She replied, "Your signet and your cord, and the staff that is in your hand." So he gave them to her, and went in to her, and she conceived by him. 19 Then she got up and went away, and taking off her veil she put on the garments of her widowhood.

20 When Judah sent the kid by his friend the Adullamite, to recover the pledge from the woman, he could not find her. 21 He asked the townspeople, "Where is the temple prostitute who was at Enaim by the wayside?" But they said, "No prostitute has been here." 22 So he returned to Judah, and said, "I have not found her; moreover the townspeople said, 'No prostitute has been here.'" 23 Judah replied, "Let her keep the things as her own, otherwise we will be laughed at; you see, I sent this kid, and you could not find her."

24 About three months later Judah was told, "Your daughter-in-law Tamar has played the whore; moreover she is pregnant as a result of whoredom." And Judah said, "Bring her out, and let her be burned."

25 As she was being brought out, she sent word to her father-in-law, "It was the owner of these who made me pregnant." And she said, "Take note, please, whose these are, the signet and the cord and the staff." 26 Then Judah acknowledged them and said, "She is more in the

right than I, since I did not give her to my son Shelah." And he did not lie with her again.

²⁷ When the time of her delivery came, there were twins in her womb.

²⁸ While she was in labor, one put out a hand; and the midwife took and bound on his hand a crimson thread, saying, "This one came out first." ²⁹ But just then he drew back his hand, and out came his brother; and she said, "What a breach you have made for yourself!" Therefore he was named Perez. ³⁰ Afterward his brother came out with the crimson thread on his hand; and he was named Zerah.

Why Judah?

We must not be surprised to find at this point in the story of Joseph a tale about the early years of Judah. He too has an important part to play alongside Joseph in what God is now going to do to bring Jacob's family back to himself as the consequences of that fateful day at Dothan work themselves out. Joseph certainly takes the lead in opening up new possibilities of life for his brothers. He gives a faithful witness to God and calls them to come back to him. He saves them from possible slavery and starvation. But at the critical moment, when Joseph had done everything he could in the service of God, the success of his work will be seen also to depend on Judah. It is Judah who will lead his brothers in the way of repentance towards God. It will be Judah who alone in the whole family finds the words that express what the human heart should feel in its penitential return. It will be Judah, too, who manages to break down Joseph's own heart after it becomes too unyielding to the need for mercy, and to the truth of mercy (cf. pp. 71ff.).

21

His faith in God was to develop gradually. Yet slowly, during the twenty years, while Joseph was serving out his long term of slavery and was being prepared for his high position in Egypt, God was also at work with this other man in the old home in Canaan, gradually bringing him to his senses, shaping his experience towards the moment when he would be able to make his decisive intervention in the developing history of the family, and fitting him ultimately to take over its leadership.

Male Authority

His early career was by no means propitious. Having cut himself loose from his family circle, he had become very familiar with the people of the land, had thrown himself into their social life, and had made a special friend of Hirah the Adullamite. Looking around locally for a wife, he had married Shua the daughter of a certain Canaanite. She had borne him three sons. As a wife for his eldest son Er he had chosen a Canaanite girl called Tamar. Er led a disreputable life, and he died childless; people believed he was struck down by God for his wickedness. Tamar was left a widow.

By local custom, and by his own family's tradition, it was the duty of Judah's next son Onan to take Tamar as his wife. Onan was rebellious against the authority that had forced him into such a marriage; he resented the union and refused on the marriage bed to give his wife a child. He too met his death prematurely and strangely. Tamar was widowed again. Judah kept her waiting, promising her his youngest son when he came of age. But when this boy Shelah had grown up, Judah began to change his mind on the matter. Possibly he had begun to imagine that Tamar might be somewhat to blame for what had happened to his other sons. Possibly, mixing so much with the Canaanites, he had begun to share some of their superstitions and fears about such cases.

Finally he put off making a decision. He kept the girl waiting on and on. He thus broke faith not only with the girl herself but with her family and with the local community, who expected more than fickleness from someone of Judah's family background. To understand the position and the story, we have to appreciate the fact that Judah had both his son and his daughter-in-law completely in his power. Tamar had no liberty to marry into another family as long as Judah held her under this obligation to wait. It was unreasonable to hold her legally if he did not intend his son for her. His fault lay in the abuse of this extraordinary power over the young woman. As Calvin put it: "He kept one bound whom he intended to defraud." Of course the matter became a public scandal. There are other examples in the Patriarchal stories where the morality of God's people shows up badly amongst their heathen neighbors (cf. Gen. 12:17-20; 26:8-11). But in Judah's case his offense in public esteem is far worse than any given by Abraham or Isaac.

Male Lust

Such was the indignation among Tamar's family and friends that a plot was made. We accept Luther's legitimate suggestion that it was made not by Tamar alone but with the connivance of others in the local community. Judah was well known and closely watched, and it is doubtful if the plot could have been carried out by a single person trying to act in secrecy. Judah, we should note, betrays the same kind of naïveté we have seen in his father. He is easily fooled. The kind of plot they laid shows how well they knew their man, and how little they respected him because of what they knew. It was obvious that this was not the kind of neighborhood in which one would expect a harlot to keep house, but they knew from Judah's talk how he could indulge his lust when given his opportunity, especially away from home. Thus it happened that when he was in their vicinity to shear his sheep, they dressed up Tamar to play the part. She was to lure him into a house and trap him into intercourse.

Commentators note how the details of the affair tell against Judah, how the story stresses the completely uncontrolled promiscuousness and indiscriminate nature of his lust. "He sees the woman at a distance," says Calvin, "and it is not possible that he should be captivated by her beauty." Bishop Hall notes that "neither did he see the face of her whom he lusted after. It was motive enough that she was a woman." Tamar therefore does not need to use any form of personal enticement to make the whole affair succeed. We are meant to reserve our judgment about her till the outcome tells us whether or not she has justice on her side. All she knows about herself is that she has been wronged cruelly, and she is now driven to make a public protest against a crying injustice. She is claiming her civil right to become a mother within the family that has adopted her. It is possible that she is also championing the rights of others held down like herself. She can be thought of as the forerunner of others in later times who found that the only way to move a society dominated by males was to do the unusual thing.

Luther asks us to note how chastely she behaves throughout the whole incident, and with what genuine piety and faith she acts: "It is clear that Tamar is an upright and honorable woman, for she is not proud nor does she prostitute herself to others. She seeks no illicit pleasures. She makes it her aim to become a mother in this house into which she has been placed by divine authority. Therefore she lays aside the garments she had put on, clothes herself again in the garments of widowhood and sits in mourning. Although she had been made pregnant she wants a further blessing from the Lord." To her there is nothing of which she should be ashamed. She has simply allowed this great man Judah to express himself, trusting that God in heaven would in the end be a merciful judge and show where righteousness lay.

The Exposure of a Weakling

In a series of deft and subtle strokes the narrator shows us how Judah, having sunk so low, unwittingly makes himself an object of further public ridicule in an area where there have already been many quiet witnesses to his folly. When she seduces him, Tamar, knowing how little he is to be trusted, demands from him his signet, cord, and staff as pledges to be redeemed when he will send a kid from his flock in payment for her favor (vv. 16ff.). Not suspecting her for a moment, he consents. "There is no passion which doth not for a time bereave a man of himself," comments Bishop Hall. The story takes a new turn when Judah tries to recover what he has surrendered. Obviously he is ashamed of what he has done; he wants his indiscretion kept secret. He tries to hide his identity. His friend Hirah, acting as go-between, inquires discreetly into the whereabouts of a "harlot" in the area, and an indignant community sends the indignant reply that no harlot would ever be tolerated in their midst. Judah is thus rebuked (as Abraham and Isaac were rebuked in their day), for imagining that outside his own home area people generally have low moral standards. He then gives up the quest in case his indiscretion is found out. He does not know that he is already being laughed at.

Then comes the news: Tamar is pregnant! Her fate is in Judah's hands. He has held her in his power as a member of his family. He has the power now to decide her punishment. The community gathers to hear the verdict, for it is they who have to execute the sentence. The case is decided in Tamar's absence; it was not necessary to hear such a woman before sentence. Judah on the bench now becomes upright and religious. He cannot tolerate such a thing in his household. The sentence is the most severe possible. She is to be burned! As Bishop Hall puts it: "News is brought to him that Tamar begins to swell with conception; and how he swells with rage and calls her forth to the flame like a righteous judge, without so much as staying for the time of her deliverance." We are reminded here of how harsh we can be when we make our judgments on others for the same faults we tolerate in ourselves!

We must pay tribute to the courage and skill with which Tamar won her victory and exposed him. She held herself in till the situation was as tense as possible, till Judah had played all his cards and committed himself irrevocably to the execution of the sentence. Then: *"Whose are these,"* she asked, *"the signet and the cord and the staff? By the man to whom these belong I am with child"* (v. 25, RSV). In one of his letters, the Russian writer Gogol said: "Pray to God . . . someone should so disgrace you in the sight of others that you would not know how to hide yourself for shame. . . . That man would be your true deliverer. Ah, how we need at times a slap on the face in public, given in front of all." Here is Judah given such a slap, and in the sight of the whole onlooking population! But while he bows to public opinion and admits that Tamar has won the case against him, he astutely manages to cover up most of his shame, and like Saul in a similar situation (cf. 1 Sam. 15:30) tries to preserve what remnants of human dignity he hopes might remain in him. He mentions only one of the faults that have been exposed, for he has a completely blind eye to all the others!

Obviously if he had been a true man and really repented he would have offered before all present to take her place in the fire! Obviously if he had been living his life with any fear — or even with a thought — of God, some hint of his religion would have come out in his spontaneous self-expression at such a time! We cannot help contrasting his lame self-accusation with King David's immediate confession when his own sin was exposed in public: "I have sinned against the Lord" (2 Sam. 12:13). Judah has at this time no sense of God and no clue to the way of true repentance. The writer has achieved his purpose in giving this impression of Judah. *This* is the man in whom God is going to work so marvelously! Though it is a dismal story, the last remark of the writer before he gets back to Joseph is meant to point to the future with real hope: *"He did not lie with her again."* Of course it may have been simply in deference to public opinion that Judah began to behave himself. But it is possible that the affair has led him towards a higher respect for womanhood, and that he is beginning to live with some fear of God. Where this begins, repentance can at least begin.

The Vindication of Tamar

To say of Tamar, as Judah did, *"She is more in the right than I"* (v. 26) is to damn with faint praise. This story is told not only to show how sordid Judah was, but also to show how great and pleasing to God was the woman of belligerent faith. She gives birth to two sons. One of them was Perez. Among those who are listed among the sons of Judah who finally emigrated to Egypt these two are both named. Tamar's children are indeed to be numbered with the people of God. In his genealogy of Jesus Christ, the Gospel writer Luke includes "Perez, the son of Judah" (Luke 3:33). Matthew, who also mentions three women in Christ's lineage, includes Tamar herself (Matt. 1:3).

We have already noted Tamar's hatred of wrong, her readiness to challenge people who practice injustice and the system that supports their cruelty. Her story reminds us of a book published a couple of generations back on the prophet Amos, titled *A Cry for Justice*. It reminds us too of a parable Jesus spoke in praise of a woman who, crushed by law, pestered a judge night and day to be "avenged" of her adversary. "Shall not God avenge his own elect?" Jesus said (Luke 18:7). We have also noted Tamar's skill in dealing with the situation. She had an almost divine insight into the character of the fool she was exposing, and she did her work imaginatively in the midst of extreme personal risk.

Tamar's heart was all the time in the right place. This is why she was forgiven for whatever today may seem dubious in her method.

What she did was done by faith. The reason she was so concerned to have offspring was not simply to be a mother, or to achieve social standing, but — in contrast to Judah and his brothers — to find an active place for herself and her children among the descendants of Abraham and under the shelter of their God. She would have been on the side of Joseph had she been a lineal daughter of Jacob. She saw, prized, and wanted in their family tradition what Judah and his brothers despised and rejected. Moreover, she believed that God had called her out of her heathen world to share in her own way in the blessing promised for all nations. She is the first of three outstanding women in the Bible who, coming from a heathen background, put their trust in the God of Israel. Her faith was accepted and honored like that of Ruth the Moabitess. A New Testament writer wrote in admiration of another heathen woman: "By faith Rahab the harlot did not perish with those who were disobedient" (Heb. 11:31). The same writer could have included Tamar along with Gideon, David, Samuel, and others who "through faith conquered kingdoms, enforced justice, received promises, stopped the mouths of lions, quenched raging fire, escaped the edge of the sword, won strength out of weakness and became mighty in war" (Heb. 11:32-34).

CHAPTER 4

Joseph Adopts Egypt and Finds Favor

Genesis 39:1–40:23

39 Now Joseph was taken down to Egypt, and Potiphar, an officer of Pharaoh, the captain of the guard, an Egyptian, bought him from the Ishmaelites who had brought him down there. 2 The Lord was with Joseph, and he became a successful man; he was in the house of his Egyptian master. 3 His master saw that the Lord was with him, and that the Lord caused all that he did to prosper in his hands. 4 So Joseph found favor in his sight and attended him; he made him overseer of his house and put him in charge of all that he had. 5 From the time that he made him overseer in his house and over all that he had, the Lord blessed the Egyptian's house for Joseph's sake; the blessing of the Lord was on all that he had, in house and field. 6 So he left all that he had in Joseph's charge; and, with him there, he had no concern for anything but the food that he ate.

Now Joseph was handsome and good-looking. 7 And after a time his master's wife cast her eyes on Joseph and said, "Lie with me." 8 But he refused and said to his master's wife, "Look, with me here, my master has no concern about anything in the house, and he has put everything that he has in my hand. 9 He is not greater in this house than I am, nor has he kept back anything from me except yourself, because you are his wife. How then could I do this great wickedness, and sin

29

against God?" 10 And although she spoke to Joseph day after day, he would not consent to lie beside her or to be with her. 11 One day, however, when he went into the house to do his work, and while no one else was in the house, 12 she caught hold of his garment, saying, "Lie with me!" But he left his garment in her hand and fled and ran outside. 13 When she saw that he had left his garment in her hand and had fled outside, 14 she called out to the members of her household and said to them, "See, my husband has brought among us a Hebrew to insult us! He came in to me to lie with me, and I cried out with a loud voice; 15 and when he heard me raise my voice and cry out, he left his garment beside me, and fled outside." 16 Then she kept his garment by her until his master came home, 17 and she told him the same story, saying, "The Hebrew servant, whom you have brought among us, came in to me to insult me; 18 but as soon as I raised my voice and cried out, he left his garment beside me, and fled outside."

19 When his master heard the words that his wife spoke to him, saying, "This is the way your servant treated me," he became enraged. 20 And Joseph's master took him and put him into the prison, the place where the king's prisoners were confined; he remained there in prison. 21 But the Lord was with Joseph and showed him steadfast love; he gave him favor in the sight of the chief jailer. 22 The chief jailer committed to Joseph's care all the prisoners who were in the prison, and whatever was done there, he was the one who did it. 23 The chief jailer paid no heed to anything that was in Joseph's care, because the Lord was with him; and whatever he did, the Lord made it prosper.

40 Sometime after this, the cupbearer of the king of Egypt and his baker offended their lord the king of Egypt. 2 Pharaoh was angry with his two officers, the chief cupbearer and the chief baker, 3 and he put them in custody in the house of the captain of the guard, in the prison where Joseph was confined. 4 The captain of the guard charged Joseph with them, and he waited on them; and they continued for some time in custody. 5 One night they both dreamed — the cupbearer and the baker of the king of Egypt, who were confined in the prison — each his own dream, and each dream with its own meaning. 6 When Joseph came to them in the morning, he saw that they were troubled. 7 So he asked Pharaoh's officers, who were with him in custody in his master's house, "Why are your faces downcast today?" 8 They said to him, "We have had dreams, and there is no one to interpret them." And Joseph said to them, "Do not interpretations belong to God? Please tell them to me."

9 So the chief cupbearer told his dream to Joseph, and said to him, "In my dream there was a vine before me, 10 and on the vine there were three branches. As soon as it budded, its blossoms came out and the clusters ripened into grapes. 11 Pharaoh's cup was in my hand; and I took the grapes and pressed them into Pharaoh's cup, and placed the cup in Pharaoh's hand." 12 Then Joseph said to him, "This is its interpretation: the three branches are three days; 13 within three days Pharaoh will lift up your head and restore you to your office; and you shall place Pharaoh's cup in his hand, just as you used to do when you were his cupbearer. 14 But remember me when it is well with you; please do me the kindness to make mention of me to Pharaoh, and so get me out of this place. 15 For in fact I was stolen out of the land of the Hebrews; and here also I have done nothing that they should have put me into the dungeon."

16 When the chief baker saw that the interpretation was favorable, he said to Joseph, "I also had a dream; there were three cake baskets on my head, 17 and in the uppermost basket there were all sorts of baked food for Pharaoh, but the birds were eating it out of the basket on my head." 18 And Joseph answered, "This is the interpretation; the three baskets are three days; 19 within three days Pharaoh will lift up your head — from you! — and hang you on a pole; and the birds will eat the flesh from you."

20 On the third day, which was Pharaoh's birthday, he made a feast for all his servants, and lifted up the head of the chief cupbearer and the chief baker among his servants. 21 He restored the chief cupbearer to his cupbearing, and he placed the cup in Pharaoh's hand; 22 but the

chief baker he hanged, just as Joseph had interpreted to them. [23] Yet the chief cupbearer did not remember Joseph, but forgot him.

Joseph Tested and Triumphant

In each of these two chapters, the writer has one main purpose in mind. He wants to tell us where and how Joseph was able to come through the threat of death, the shock of humiliation, the torture of being chained as a slave and sold into Egypt, and how he further reacted when having at first found good fortune in Egypt he had it suddenly wrenched from him, to find himself again in the depths. From the fascinating detail in the encounter with Potiphar's wife we are given a clear though brief glimpse of the power and source of the faith that had enabled Joseph to stand firm in the earlier phase of his deep trouble. The further account of how he applied himself in the Egyptian prison to the study of dreams, and won the confidence of Pharaoh, gives us our first glimpse of his positive determination in Egypt to overcome all adversity and to command respect.

Moreover, as we read through both chapters we discover how naturally gifted and attractive a person Joseph really was. He has outgrown completely the immature faults that show up too easily in the hostile and restraining atmosphere of his home. Here in Egypt, able to be himself as one among others on an even pitch, he is outstanding. Describing the personal influence and charm of a great actress of fifty years ago a recent article says that "when she was there you knew you were in the presence of somebody." Joseph was not only able to impress people like Potiphar and the jail guard; he inspired their trust and proved he had the ability to deserve it in all circumstances, whatever the task. He was obviously the friend and favorite of ordinary people around him, and he must have been extremely tactful with those over whom he was given control. If only the brothers had allowed him freedom to be himself at home! It reminds us again of the irrationality of their hatred, and calls on us afresh to reexamine some of our dislikes.

It is in the spontaneous reply to Potiphar's wife when she tempted him: *"How can I do this great wickedness and sin against God?"* (v. 9) that we have the clearest revelation, not simply of Joseph's theological and moral convictions, but of his deep, constant, and living piety. His morality was based not just in his beliefs about God but on his close experience of fellowship with God. We can glimpse here the sense of God's presence that always dominated his attitude and behavior, a point we should dwell on if we are fully to understand him. Though Joseph often speaks theologically in a profound way, he does not often speak piously, and throughout the whole account we are not shown him often actually at prayer, either by himself or with others. Yet we should not underestimate at any stage in his life the power and genuineness of his religious experience. No doubt his dreams were given to him at the heart of an experience of God's personal presence similar to Solomon's when the "Lord appeared to him in a dream by night" (1 Kings 3:5).

One of the psalms, in an outline of important and decisive early incidents in the history of Israel, tells us that when Joseph was being enslaved, when "his feet were hurt with fetters" and "his neck was put in a collar of iron," this "Word of the Lord" was on his mind and "kept testing him." We can imagine the desperate questions he must have asked himself. Why this? What was the purpose of the God of his fathers in putting him through this? Yet he did not doubt, the psalm assures us, that what God had spoken would come to pass (105:19). It is possible that at some stage during the early period in Egypt his mind would turn to the strange dream God gave his ancestor Abraham in a deep sleep, when "terrifying darkness" came upon him: "Know this for certain, that your offspring shall be aliens in a land that is not theirs and they shall be slaves there and shall be oppressed for four hundred years, but I will bring judgment on the nation that they serve and afterwards they shall come out with great possessions" (Gen. 15:13-15). We can well imagine him linking his own experience in some way with this Word.

All the evidence from the story indicates that he had imbibed through the family tradition the same trustful commitment to God of all the difficulties he faced, as Abraham had taught those around him (cf., e.g., Gen. 24:12ff.); and it was this living piety practiced in the midst of the affairs entrusted to him by Potiphar and the head jailer that enabled God to make him in their eyes a "successful man" (39:2). When, later on, he said to his brothers, "I fear God" (42:18), this was the kind of piety he was referring to. When he found himself in chains and slavery he no doubt found such simple faith deeply tested, and he had to struggle to hold on to the Word, which nevertheless held him in its grip and brought him to the radiant conviction that all things — even those which are against us — are for us, and that God makes them work together for good to those who love him (Rom. 8:28).

It is worth remembering that the temptation he encountered with Potiphar's wife was a test to him to give evidence, not just of his faithfulness and reliability to a human master who had trusted him with all his affairs; it was much more a crucial test of whether he had kept his zeal and love for God entire and pure. His reply to her, *"How can I do this great wickedness and sin against God?"* (v. 9), is a reminder to us that not only the sin of actual adultery but the type of free sexual lust to which she was tempting him was then, and still is, abhorrent to the God we know in Christ, and can hinder our ability to be of service to him in his kingdom.

As we watch him further, especially during his imprisonment in Egypt, we discover how, in his own deep suffering (and at this point he was in the midst of it!) he had resisted all temptation to brood over his hard fate, and had allowed his suffering to make him sympathetic with others rather than bitter. It is here in prison that we are able to catch one of the warmest and most intimate glimpses of the kind of person he blossomed into among normal people, as he interpreted the dreams of Pharaoh's butler and baker. He had obviously already won their confidence, and when he saw them looking more downcast and worried than usual his deep and genuine concern revealed itself: he simply asked what was wrong. They had already found in him the kind of sympathy that made them feel they could confide in him; they must have viewed him as a friend. No doubt it was this human sympathy as much as his interpretive skill that brought him back to the butler's memory at the crucial moment.

"In the World But Not of It"

During a famine in Canaan many years before, Abraham too had spent some time journeying in Egypt. While there he had feared for his own safety. Sarah was an exceptionally beautiful woman, and he had heard that Egyptian men were apt to murder any pilgrims who came their way if they wanted their wives. So he avoided the supposed danger to his life by passing Sarah off everywhere as his sister. In the end he was rebuked by the king of Egypt for allowing such a ludicrous tale about foreigners to enter his mind.

Joseph had no such "hang-ups." Egypt, he believed, was where God had sent him for a purpose he was yet to discover, and in settling there he felt he was under the providence, and could indeed be in the presence, of the God of his fathers. As long as he was not asked to sin against God he believed he was doing right to conform to its ways and customs and culture. The Egyptians were religious. They spoke often about God and Joseph spoke freely with them as they did so, even though he knew that the word for "God" brought up quite different ideas in their minds than in his own. What attracted him especially and drew him most strongly to the heart of this culture was, however, the high place given everywhere to the study of "Wisdom." This was a largely secular pursuit. It involved the study of the virtues and skills a man needed to live well and successfully (especially in high places in court circles). It offered an understanding of the meaning of life, and taught how to lead and counsel others to follow the best paths. The royal court had its council of wise men whom the king consulted. This wisdom, full of precepts, adages, poems, and songs, was collected into books. The Bible contains typical books of Wisdom, some of the thinking, language, and imagery of which were directly borrowed from the Egyptian books of the time of Solomon. We can well imagine Joseph, facing an indefinite term of imprisonment in Egypt, settling down to master this literature while he had the time and opportunity. One very important task fulfilled by such wise men in Egypt was the interpretation of dreams. Our story indicates that Joseph made a special study of this practice as it had prevailed in Egypt for centuries, perhaps looking for a confirmation of his own personal experience of the Word of God that had come through his own dreams.

Yet even in interpreting dreams Joseph never forgot his own dream — much more important than any others brought before him in Egypt — his dream about the purpose he was to fulfill among the people of God, on their way to become a blessing to all nations! Thus, while he settled down in Egypt under the providence of God, on his vizier's throne and horse, dressed and acting properly as a traditional Egyptian potentate, he could never forget that he was not an Egyptian and could never become a real one. We are meant to take special note of one gesture, highly significant of his inward alienation of mind and heart. To his two sons by the daughter of an Egyptian priest he gave not Egyptian but Hebrew names — each with a prophetic meaning that was to be fully understood only when their descendants took their place among the tribes of Israel in the Exodus wanderings and the final settlement in the promised land (see p. 57).

"The Lord . . . Gave Him Favor"

In our exposition of this passage we have already noted that Joseph was a naturally favored person. We have dwelt on the gifts and qualities that helped to win him popularity — his personal charm and ready sympathy. We have mentioned, too, his outstanding reliability of character. He inspired trust in those who had responsibility for affairs of real importance, and he proved himself always deserving of it.

When the writer mentions, however, that *"the Lord"* in his steadfast love to Joseph gave him *"favor"* in the sight of the chief jailer (39:21), what is being referred to is something extra and quite special. By a movement of grace in the hearts and minds of those around him, God gave Joseph's contemporaries an uncommon inclination towards him. The most apt language we can use here is found in a prophecy about the favor God will show Israel in the last days, drawing all nations to her. Addressing Israel, God promises that even "nations that do not know you will hasten to you, because of the Lord your God, the Holy One of Israel, for he has *endowed you with splendor*" (Isa. 55:5, NIV; the RSV has "he has glorified you"). What had happened already with Potiphar in the earlier phase of Joseph's house-stewardship, and with the jailer in his prison, is going to continue. God is going to so "endow Joseph with splendor" in the eyes of Pharaoh and his wise men that they will ask their people to believe he is the kind of man through whom God will bring true blessing to the whole life of their community. We are reminded of how God made the skin of Moses' face to shine, though he was not aware of it (Exod. 34:29).

We are reminded again here of how often in the Bible story God is shown powerfully working his purposes in world history not by waging war, or by instigating social or political revolution, but in quiet unobtrusive ways. "The kingdom of God is not coming by things that can be observed" (Luke 17:20). Often he achieves his will simply by creating "favor" in people's hearts and minds. It was because he inclined Cyrus the Persian emperor to give favor to Israel, at the end of their period of exile, that they were rescued from Babylon and given the liberty to go back to their homeland (Isa. 44:26–45:13). "The king's heart is a stream of water in the hand of the Lord; he turns it wherever he will" (Prov. 21:1). The same quiet miracle of a king's heart inclined to give favor is about to take place in Egypt.

We accept the suggestion of a recent scholar (whose name I have regretfully lost) on the passage before us, that the influence God gave to Joseph was a foretaste of the blessing God promised Abraham would be passed on to the world. "Joseph," he says, "has the blessing, and upon everything he does the blessing rests. And from the story of his life it becomes clear that this blessing is not given to make him and his family happy. It is rather in very truth the great blessing of Abraham, through which the Creator and Redeemer will bless all nations of the earth and redeem them from corruption. Joseph, sold by his brothers' hatred and envy into a strange land, saves not only Israel but Egypt also. That is a prophetic prelude to the salvation of the world by the suffering of the servant of God, Israel, which is grounded and fulfilled in the One Brother who, rejected by all the sons of Israel, was sold for thirty pieces of silver, Christ Jesus."

Some Relevant Reflections

What has been brought out of the story in these two chapters can be seen as closely relevant to our church situation today. During the early years of my ministry in the United Kingdom, sixty years ago, we had no doubt that the Christian faith deserved a favored place as the "established" religion of our land. We called ourselves a "Christian country" and expected our laws and social customs to reflect especially what we regarded as uniquely Christian moral convictions. We spoke confidently about the absolute finality of Christ, and we tended to regard any other religion as "heathen." The gospel was to be absolutely trusted as Joseph was in his day in Egypt. We believed it could easily be proved that the teaching and social influence of the Christian faith over centuries of progress had had a far more elevating and beneficial influence in our Western culture than any of the other great world religions had had over the lands in which they had been accepted. We felt it was our duty to seek to convert and elevate the world through our foreign mission enterprise. Now, of course, much has radically changed. We are reminded often that we are a "pluralistic society" in which no religion should seek any form of preference or favor for its tenets or teaching. We are called on to be content as Christians to demote ourselves to one alongside other equals. Moreover, it is often claimed that our attempts at foreign missions were too closely allied with imperialistic political aims and in the long run achieved as much harm as the good we so fondly intended. Many around us are cutting themselves loose from what were once regarded as settled Christian moral convictions, because they believe the gospel has failed even in the reliability test.

It is my belief that even demoted from its absolute position and laid alongside others as a "religion" or a "creed" or a "way of life," Christianity is still vastly superior to all else and "worthy of full acceptance" (1 Tim. 1:15; 4:9), indeed of all "favor"! We need not be ashamed of having accepted and benefited from our now rejected favored status. We need, however, have no regret or fear as we face the future with our former secure popularity on the wane. During the years of our establishment we yielded too often to the temptation to make our gospel conform to the thought-forms and tastes of the world around us, and we were too ready to cover over those aspects of the Cross that gave offense to the natural mind. We can now begin to understand by experience what Paul meant when he spoke of himself as being "crucified to the world." Moreover, we are beginning to discover as never before that the foolishness of the gospel is truly our wisdom, and its weakness is our strength (cf. 1 Cor. 1:27-28).

It is as we are now, of course, that we may find God still powerfully at work in our midst, giving his "favor" to those who are "not ashamed" (Rom. 1:16) — and still ready, as he promised, to "endow" his church with a "splendor" far beyond anything we had through our being "established" (cf. Acts 6:15; 2 Cor. 3:18).

CHAPTER 5

Joseph Exalted

Genesis 41:1-57

41 After two whole years, Pharaoh dreamed that he was standing by the Nile, [2] and there came up out of the Nile seven sleek and fat cows, and they grazed in the reed grass. [3] Then seven other cows, ugly and thin, came up out of the Nile after them, and stood by the other cows on the bank of the Nile. [4] The ugly and thin cows ate up the seven sleek and fat cows. And Pharaoh awoke. [5] Then he fell asleep and dreamed a second time; seven ears of grain, plump and good, were growing on one stalk. [6] Then seven ears, thin and blighted by the east wind, sprouted after them. [7] The thin ears swallowed up the seven plump and full ears. Pharaoh awoke, and it was a dream. [8] In the morning his spirit was troubled; so he sent and called for all the magicians of Egypt and all its wise men. Pharaoh told them his dreams, but there was no one who could interpret them to Pharaoh.

[9] Then the chief cupbearer said to Pharaoh, "I remember my faults today. [10] Once Pharaoh was angry with his servants, and put me and the chief baker in custody in the house of the captain of the guard. [11] We dreamed on the same night, he and I, each having a dream with its own meaning. [12] A young Hebrew was there with us, a servant of the captain of the guard. When we told him, he interpreted our dreams to us, giving an interpretation to each according to his dream. [13] As he in-

41

terpreted to us, so it turned out; I was restored to my office, and the baker was hanged."

14 Then Pharaoh sent for Joseph, and he was hurriedly brought out of the dungeon. When he had shaved himself and changed his clothes, he came in before Pharaoh. 15 And Pharaoh said to Joseph, "I have had a dream, and there is no one who can interpret it. I have heard it said of you that when you hear a dream you can interpret it." 16 Joseph answered Pharaoh, "It is not I; God will give Pharaoh a favorable answer." 17 Then Pharaoh said to Joseph, "In my dream I was standing on the banks of the Nile; 18 and seven cows, fat and sleek, came up out of the Nile and fed in the reed grass. 19 Then seven other cows came up after them, poor, very ugly, and thin. Never had I seen such ugly ones in all the land of Egypt. 20 The thin and ugly cows ate up the first seven cows, 21 but when they had eaten them no one would have known that they had done so, for they were still as ugly as before. Then I awoke. 22 I fell asleep a second time and I saw in my dream seven ears of grain, full and good, growing on one stalk, 23 and seven ears, withered, thin, and blighted by the east wind, sprouting after them; 24 and the thin ears swallowed up the seven good ears. But when I told it to the magicians, there was no one who could explain it to me."

25 Then Joseph said to Pharaoh, "Pharaoh's dreams are one and the same; God has revealed to Pharaoh what he is about to do. 26 The seven good cows are seven years, and the seven good ears are seven years; the dreams are one. 27 The seven lean and ugly cows that came up after them are seven years, as are the seven empty ears blighted by the east wind; they are seven years of famine. 28 It is as I told Pharaoh; God has shown to Pharaoh what he is about to do. 29 There will come seven years of great plenty throughout all the land of Egypt. 30 After them there will arise seven years of famine, and all the plenty will be forgotten in the land of Egypt; the famine will consume the land. 31 The plenty will no longer be known in the land because of the famine that will follow, for it will be very grievous. 32 And the doubling of

Pharaoh's dream means that the thing is fixed by God, and God will shortly bring it about. 33 Now therefore let Pharaoh select a man who is discerning and wise, and set him over the land of Egypt. 34 Let Pharaoh proceed to appoint overseers over the land, and take one-fifth of the produce of the land of Egypt during the seven plenteous years. 35 Let them gather all the food of these good years that are coming, and lay up grain under the authority of Pharaoh for food in the cities, and let them keep it. 36 That food shall be a reserve for the land against the seven years of famine that are to befall the land of Egypt, so that the land may not perish through the famine."

37 The proposal pleased Pharaoh and all his servants. 38 Pharaoh said to his servants, "Can we find anyone else like this — one in whom is the spirit of God?" 39 So Pharaoh said to Joseph, "Since God has shown you all this, there is no one so discerning and wise as you. 40 You shall be over my house, and all my people shall order themselves as you command; only with regard to the throne will I be greater than you." 41 And Pharaoh said to Joseph, "See, I have set you over all the land of Egypt." 42 Removing his signet ring from his hand, Pharaoh put it on Joseph's hand; he arrayed him in garments of fine linen, and put a gold chain around his neck. 43 He had him ride in the chariot of his second-in-command; and they cried out in front of him, "Bow the knee!" Thus he set him over all the land of Egypt. 44 Moreover Pharaoh said to Joseph, "I am Pharaoh, and without your consent no one shall lift up hand or foot in all the land of Egypt." 45 Pharaoh gave Joseph the name Zaphenath-paneah; and he gave him Asenath daughter of Potiphera, priest of On, as his wife. Thus Joseph gained authority over the land of Egypt.

46 Joseph was thirty years old when he entered the service of Pharaoh king of Egypt. And Joseph went out from the presence of Pharaoh, and went through all the land of Egypt. 47 During the seven plenteous years the earth produced abundantly. 48 He gathered up all the food of the seven years when there was plenty in the land of Egypt, and stored up food in the cities; he stored up in every city the food from

the fields around it. ⁴⁹ So Joseph stored up grain in such abundance —
like the sand of the sea — that he stopped measuring it; it was beyond
measure.

⁵⁰ Before the years of famine came, Joseph had two sons, whom
Asenath daughter of Potiphera, priest of On, bore to him. ⁵¹ Joseph
named the first-born Manasseh, "For," he said, "God has made me forget all my hardship and all my father's house." ⁵² The second he
named Ephraim, "For God has made me fruitful in the land of my
misfortunes."

⁵³ The seven years of plenty that prevailed in the land of Egypt
came to an end; ⁵⁴ and the seven years of famine began to come, just as
Joseph had said. There was famine in every country, but throughout
the land of Egypt there was bread. ⁵⁵ When all the land of Egypt was
famished, and the people cried to Pharaoh for bread, Pharaoh said to
all the Egyptians, "Go to Joseph; what he says to you, do." ⁵⁶ And since
the famine had spread over all the land, Joseph opened all the store-
houses, and sold to the Egyptians, for the famine was severe in the
land of Egypt. ⁵⁷ Moreover, all the world came to Joseph in Egypt to
buy grain, because the famine became severe throughout the world.

How God Makes World History

We have been waiting from chapter to chapter for Joseph's release
and vindication. Now we discover why we have had to wait so long. A
catastrophic famine is going to threaten both Egypt and the surrounding nations. God is concerned that human suffering should be
avoided. He is engaged in making world history, as well as in working out Joseph's history. Pharaoh had to be made ready to dream his
dreams, and ready for Joseph too.

Pharaoh at the time he dreamed his dream had obviously become hard-pressed by the responsibility of having to rule people — and he felt the loneliness of his throne. Demosthenes, speaking of the burden an earthly ruler has to bear, once said that if he were offered a choice between two ways, one leading to death, the other to civil administration, he would choose the way that led to death! When the two famous dreams came, Pharaoh felt that his burden was now becoming insupportable, and he longed for someone with whom to share it. He wanted a man who could first of all explain to him the mystery of what he had seen. Why did they appear in sevens? — seven cows, seven ears? Why should these gaunt cattle so greedily consume the fat cattle? Why should seven plump and full ears have been replaced by the lean and withered ears? He was convinced that there was some urgent message for him to hear. He was convinced, too, that the true explanation was simple and straightforward. He almost had it himself! He would recognize it as soon as he heard it. If only someone could give him the clue! He looked in vain for this man among his own official dream interpreters and wise men. They told him what the symbolism of such dreams normally meant; they set up a special committee and brought him their report. They quoted the books of the sages. They showed him historical precedents. But all they could do was to suggest further avenues of thought. All this was the preparation of Pharaoh to meet Joseph!

Then suddenly the butler remembered, with a twinge of conscience, the jail and the *"young Hebrew"* to whom he had owed so much! *"I remember my faults today"* (v. 9). The poor embarrassed man hardly knew why he was doing it — confessing his sins aloud, and speaking so well of the strange attractive foreign youth who had helped him in prison, and apologizing for not having thought of it sooner! Yet it would not have been so effective had he remembered it sooner. It was God who had made it happen exactly this way, and *"to-day."* Yesterday would have been too early; Pharaoh would not yet have been desperately ready, in such critical need. God brought the relief when the pressure was exactly right. And now suddenly everything fits into place. Now it all becomes *obvious:* Why years before Joseph was sold into slavery and brought to Egypt, why Pharaoh had become angry one day with his butler and had thought over it again later, why Joseph had spent so much time studying dreams and learning the ways of the court, why the butler forgot. The more we think over the details, the more we see how "in *everything*" (cf. Rom. 8:28) God has been working to bring about what happens here. Joseph seems to have been so meticulously prepared that he graduates perfectly into the new situation that awaits him. His whole career has been a rehearsal for this day! He speaks with the competence of a shrewd statesman with years of experience behind him — and indeed he is such, for God, since his birth, has been gradually making him such a man.

Suddenly, moreover, as everything fits in, the future too is decided. Without a moment's hesitation the mystery of the dream is unraveled. Pharaoh, as soon as he hears, sees it all; his burden is completely lifted. Here is the man to whom alone has been given the simple truth. Pharaoh too felt liberated at that very moment, and responded with astonishing openness and generosity. For Joseph, everything from this moment is different. "Behold," writes Bishop Hall, "one hour hath changed his fetters into a chain of gold, his rags into pure linen, his stocks into a chariot, his jail into a palace, Potiphar's captive into his master's Lord, the noise of his chains into 'Bow the knee!'"

All in "one hour" — suddenly! Suddenly at the Red Sea, the waters opened up and Israel went over. Suddenly at Carmel the fire fell from heaven on the sacrifice, and Israel was again converted. Suddenly the Holy Spirit came upon Mary, the power of the Most High overshadowed her, and she was with child. Suddenly St. Paul on the road to Damascus was confronted by the risen Jesus! Often, no doubt, God takes his time. Things seem to be allowed to slide, and if there is growth, it is slow. We must bear his delays. "With the Lord," wrote Peter, "a thousand years are like one day." We have to wait with patience for the next move. But then when certain chosen days arrive "one day is like a thousand years" (2 Peter 3:8) and what takes place in that short day can be the work of a millennium! Jesus warned us that these great days or sudden hours may come upon us at any time — especially in the day we might be least expecting it. Therefore we must always be ready and expectant — as Joseph was in this prison. We have to be faithful when what we have under our care is insignificant, for it is to those who are faithful in "little" to whom "much" is finally entrusted (Matt. 25:23). We have to remember that the great climax towards which everything is moving will come "in a moment, in the twinkling of an eye" (1 Cor. 15:52).

Here in this passage we are reminded that the key person in bringing together Pharaoh and Joseph, and in deciding so much for Egypt and Israel, was the butler. Certainly it looks as if he had to be prompted by God when the time set for his part arrived. But he is here to remind us that ordinary people have always their part to play, and that it pleases God that neither the apostles, nor the prophets, nor the kings of this world, nor the kingdom of God itself can function in a healthy way without them.

Joseph Proclaims His Faith

The apostle Paul was taken out of prison and was given an opportunity to argue his case before King Agrippa and the assembly of distinguished people who had gathered at Caesarea to discuss important affairs of state. But he forgot his own cause and used the occasion to preach! He spoke of Christ so pressingly that Festus the governor interrupted him and Agrippa almost reproached him for his enthusiasm to make other people Christians. Paul accepted the rebuke and answered: "I would to God that not only you but also all who hear me this day might become such as I am — except for these chains" (Acts 26:29). To Joseph also, taken out of prison, the chance to interpret the dream was merely an opportunity for confessing and proclaiming his faith in God: *"It is not I. God will give Pharaoh a favorable answer. . . . God has shown to Pharaoh what he is about to do . . . the thing is fixed by God, and God will shortly bring it about"* (vv. 16, 28, 32). When he speaks of "God" he is speaking of the only God he knows to speak about — the God of Abraham, Isaac, and Jacob, his father's God, whom during his Egyptian captivity he has come to know even better than he had at home. Though they may not have realized it he is attempting to lift all these Egyptians out of their superstitious thought-world into his own. He is trying to take their minds off their notions of fate and chance so that they can share his own sense of providence, guidance, and stability under the kind of God who can be known and trusted — as the God of his father Israel could be known and trusted. He is affirming to Pharaoh and his court that this God is also Lord over the court of Pharaoh. It is God who has been disturbing the sleep of Pharaoh himself. It is he who has shown Joseph the meaning of the vision. It is he who will give him a favorable response for Pharaoh. The God of Abraham and of young Joseph — now in control of all the strange visions and omens that are at this time dominating the politics of this heathen land! It was the same kind of vision seen centuries later by Ezekiel in his vivid picture of another heathen king being guided in the way, directed by the God of Israel through the results of pagan augury. "For the king of Babylon stands at the parting of the way, at the head of two ways, to use divination; he shakes the arrows, he consults the teraphim, he looks at the liver. Into his right hand comes the lot for Jerusalem" (Ezek. 21:21-22).

Joseph's God called for action! The Word of God in the dream had warned of the coming years of famine. Let man believe and prepare. Discipline was required, organization was required, a good and wise leader would be required. Let Pharaoh and his court be warned — and act. "True and lawful prophets of God," observed Calvin on this speech, "do not merely predict . . . but propose remedies for impending evils."

The Miracle of Hearing

In the New Testament the apostle Paul tells of a miracle of hearing that took place when he preached the gospel in Thessalonica. The people responded immediately and whole-heartedly; with no delay they turned to God from idols! When he wrote to them later he explained why this had happened: when he preached to them they had received his word not as a merely human utterance, but as what it really is, *"the Word of God."* He thanks God that such a hearing of God's voice had happened, and points out that they could easily have received his word simply as a word of man (1 Thess. 2:13, 14). An Old Testament miracle of hearing took place in Egypt on the day of Joseph's sermon at court. Pharaoh's ears were opened by God to hear an impelling divine Word. His response was inspired no less than Joseph's own utterance.

Of course there were purely human factors both in Joseph's appeal and in the monarch's decision about him. The way Joseph stated his facts — his sincerity and clarity, his patent concern about the situation he foretold from the dream, his eminently sensible advice, the urgency of his call to action — all made their impression. But Pharaoh was moved at a level deeper than can be naturally explained. When he heard Joseph, he believed he was listening to God. Here was a voice coming from beyond and above all that was so shifting and misleading in the great Egyptian world around him. Here was no echo of his own or of another human mind. He was relieved at last from the burden of his tormenting uncertainties, and he was moved and stirred to action. "A prophet," said Jesus, "is not without honor except in his own country and in his own house" (Matt. 13:57). Rejected by his own kith and kin, Joseph was now given honor in the court of Egypt. No doubt Pharaoh had already made inquiries about him from the prison governor. Here was a man with a God he could trust, a man of conviction, charm, and obvious practical ability. Pharaoh would let him take on the leadership he had appealed for, and the responsibilities he had outlined brilliantly. He knew of no other who could do it: *"Can we find such a man as this, in whom is the spirit of God? . . . Since God has shown you all this, there is none so discreet and wise as you are; you shall be over my house, and all my people shall order themselves as you command"* (Gen. 41:38-40, RSV).

Martin Luther believed that Pharaoh was converted that day to a faith in the God of Israel, that he put his trust in God for his salvation, and that many around him also became believers. Calvin did not go so far. He believed that the Spirit of God certainly worked in the mind of Pharaoh, for the inward seal of the Spirit had given authority to his own dream. But, he argued, people can be moved by the Spirit to take a particular line of practical action in an emergency without themselves becoming thoroughly converted, and changing their entire way of life. Even people who remain essentially pagan can be moved by the Spirit to support what God is actively doing around them in the furtherance of his kingdom. They are not given by the Spirit the hope of eternal life, but they are "taught incidentally concerning the state of this present life." We prefer Calvin's estimate of what happens. We note that Pharaoh did not go the length of saying, "Can we find such a God as this?" — though he *did* say, *"Can we find such a man as this?"* (v. 38, RSV). A lasting personal relationship was thus formed between him and Joseph, that affected not only the future of Egypt, but of the people of God for many years to come.

At the Right Hand of Pharaoh

"Can we find such a man as this, in whom is the spirit of God?" This question about Joseph immediately directs our minds to Christ himself,

for he certainly is the man above all others to whom these words truly belong. Said of Joseph they bear a limited truth. Said of Jesus they remain valid even if we search the whole universe and the pages of all history. No age that may yet come will be able to cast doubt on them. They were repeated by Jesus' own disciples on the day he challenged them to desert him if they would. "Lord," they replied, "to whom shall we go?" (John 6:68).

Pharaoh's response to Joseph was lavish and extravagant as well as sudden. They brought him the best — gold and fine linen (v. 42; cf. Luke 15:22). Inspired by the Spirit, Pharaoh set no limit to Joseph's power except that it should not usurp his own (vv. 42ff.). He attached no conditions to what he gave. The description of his open generosity in this chapter is elaborated in some of its details by the writer of Psalm 105:

> The king sent and released him,
>   the ruler of the peoples set him free;
> he made him lord of his house,
>   and ruler of all his possessions,
> to instruct his officials at his pleasure,
>   and to teach his elders wisdom.
>
> (Ps. 105:20-22)

How can our minds fail to think of what God gives us in Jesus when we read all this? Of course the created world itself shows us how lavish and thorough he is in all his works. But in Christ he spares no cost — he freely gives everything (Rom. 8:32). When he frees us it is to make us great and privileged — kings and priests to God his sons! (Rev. 5:10; 1 John 3:2). When he gives us life he gives it "more abundantly" (John 10:10). "All things are yours," writes Paul, "whether . . . the world, or life, or death, or the present or the future, all are yours; and you are Christ's; and Christ is God's" (1 Cor. 3:21-23). And in doing all this God can work as suddenly as he works extravagantly! It is towards the end of our chapter with reference to what happened seven years later, that we have the greatest tributes paid to Joseph in his exaltation. When the people then cried to Pharaoh for bread, his word was: *"Go to Joseph; what he says to you do"* (v. 55). In our final verse we read, *"All the earth came to Egypt to Joseph to buy bread"* (v. 57, RSV).

We felt justified in pointing out how the descriptions of Joseph during his humiliation and rejection at home reminded us of Christ in his sufferings. Those who believe there is meaning and value in Old Testament typology find that these passages point significantly to the New Testament descriptions of Christ in his glory and exaltation. The writers of the New Testament refer often to the throne of David in the Old Testament history and in the Psalms, to find foreshadowings of the kingdom and glory of Christ. But there are hints here and there in the language they use about Jesus, that Joseph is also in their minds.

The picture we have here of the whole hungry world coming to Joseph for bread is perhaps the most significant of all we have touched on in this chapter. Jesus called all men to himself because he had everything to give them. They were to come with their need — those who were weary and heavy laden — those who thirsted for a satisfaction more lasting than anything the world could give — those who were hungry for the bread of life. He promised to disappoint no one who came. We see him in this central place in the midst of the world's need every time we come to the Lord's table. In this sacrament he shows us not only how he meets our own hunger but also how he gives the same "bread of life" to his whole church. Thus he shows us how he can meet the world's need, and how we ourselves are meant to share this bread with the whole perishing world.

CHAPTER 6

Joseph and His Brothers: The Re-encounter and After

Genesis 42:1–43:14

42 When Jacob learned that there was grain in Egypt, he said to his sons, "Why do you keep looking at one another? ²I have heard that there is grain in Egypt; go down and buy grain for us there, that we may live and not die." ³So ten of Joseph's brothers went down to buy grain in Egypt. ⁴But Jacob did not send Joseph's brother Benjamin with his brothers, for he feared that harm might come to him. ⁵Thus the sons of Israel were among the other people who came to buy grain, for the famine had reached the land of Canaan.

⁶Now Joseph was governor over the land; it was he who sold to all the people of the land. And Joseph's brothers came and bowed themselves before him with their faces to the ground. ⁷When Joseph saw his brothers, he recognized them, but he treated them like strangers and spoke harshly to them. "Where do you come from?" he said. They said, "From the land of Canaan to buy food." ⁸Although Joseph had recognized his brothers, they did not recognize him. ⁹Joseph also remembered the dreams that he had dreamed about them. He said to them, "You are spies; you have come to see the nakedness of the land!" ¹⁰They said to him, "No, my lord; your servants have come to buy food. ¹¹We are all sons of one man; we are honest men; your servants

have never been spies." 12 But he said to them, "No, you have come to see the nakedness of the land." 13 They said, "We, your servants, are twelve brothers, the sons of a certain man in the land of Canaan; the youngest, however, is now with our father, and one is no more." 14 But Joseph said to them, "It is just as I have said to you; you are spies. 15 Here is how you shall be tested; as Pharaoh lives, you shall not leave this place unless your youngest brother come here! 16 Let one of you go and bring your brother, while the rest of you remain in prison, in order that your words may be tested, whether there is truth in you; or else, as Pharaoh lives, surely you are spies." 17 And he put them all to-gether in prison for three days.

18 On the third day Joseph said to them, "Do this and you will live, for I fear God; 19 if you are honest men, let one of your brothers stay here where you are imprisoned. The rest of you shall go and carry grain for the famine of your households, 20 and bring your youngest brother to me. Thus your words will be verified, and you shall not die." And they agreed to do so. 21 They said to one another, "Alas, we are paying the penalty for what we did to our brother; we saw his anguish when he pleaded with us, but we would not listen. That is why this anguish has come upon us." 22 Then Reuben answered them, "Did I not tell you not to wrong the boy? But you would not listen. So now there comes a reckoning for his blood." 23 They did not know that Joseph understood them, since he spoke with them through an interpreter. 24 He turned away from them and wept; then he returned and spoke to them. And he picked out Simeon and had him bound before their eyes. 25 Joseph then gave orders to fill their bags with grain, to return every man's money to his sack, and to give them pro-visions for their journey. This was done for them.

26 They loaded their donkeys with their grain, and departed. 27 When one of them opened his sack to give his donkey fodder at the lodging place, he saw his money at the top of the sack. 28 He said to his brothers, "My money has been put back; here it is in my sack!" At this they lost heart and turned trembling to one another, saying, "What is this that God has done to us?"

29 When they came to their father Jacob in the land of Canaan, they told him all that had happened to them, saying, 30 "The man, the lord of the land, spoke harshly to us, and charged us with spying on the land. 31 But we said to him, 'We are honest men, we are not spies. 32 We are twelve brothers, sons of our father; one is no more, and the youngest is now with our father in the land of Canaan.' 33 Then the man, the lord of the land, said to us, 'By this I shall know that you are honest men; leave one of your brothers with me, take grain for the famine of your households, and go your way. 34 Bring your youngest brother to me, and I shall know that you are not spies but honest men. Then I will release your brother to you, and you may trade in the land.'"

35 As they were emptying their sacks, there in each one's sack was his bag of money. When they and their father saw their bundles of money, they were dismayed. 36 And their father Jacob said to them, "I am the one you have bereaved of children; Joseph is no more, and Simeon is no more, and now you would take Benjamin. All this has happened to me!" 37 Then Reuben said to his father, "You may kill my two sons if I do not bring him back to you. Put him in my hands, and I will bring him back to you." 38 But he said, "My son shall not go down with you, for his brother is dead, and he alone is left. If harm should come to him on the journey that you are to make, you would bring down my gray hairs with sorrow to Sheol."

43 Now the famine was severe in the land. 2 And when they had eaten up the grain that they had brought from Egypt, their father said to them, "Go again, buy us a little more food." 3 But Judah said to him, "The man solemnly warned us, saying, 'You shall not see my face unless your brother is with you.' 4 If you will send our brother with us, we will go down and buy you food; 5 but if you will not send him, we will not go down, for the man said to us, 'You shall not see my face, unless your brother is with you.'" 6 Israel said, "Why did you treat me so badly as to tell the man that you had another brother?" 7 They replied, "The man questioned us carefully about ourselves and our kindred, saying,

'Is your father alive? Have you another brother?' What we told him was in answer to these questions. Could we in any way know that he would say, 'Bring your brother down'?" [8] Then Judah said to his father Israel, "Send the boy with me, and let us be on our way, so that we may live and not die — you and we and also our little ones. [9] I myself will be surety for him; you can hold me accountable for him. If I do not bring him back to you and set him before you, then let me bear the blame for ever. [10] If we had not delayed, we would now have returned twice."

[11] Then their father Israel said to them, "If it must be so, then do this; take some of the choice fruits of the land in your bags, and carry them down as a present to the man — a little balm and a little honey, gum, resin, pistachio nuts, and almonds. [12] Take double the money with you. Carry back with you the money that was returned in the top of your sacks; perhaps it was an oversight. [13] Take your brother also, and be on your way again to the man; [14] may God Almighty grant you mercy before the man, so that he may send back your other brother and Benjamin. As for me, if I am bereaved of my children, I am bereaved."

Joseph Faces His Life-Work

When his brothers came to him in Egypt and bowed down before him, he had been expecting them and had prepared himself, both for the encounter and the task with which he knew he would be faced. For him it was a moment full of destiny for the future of his family and for the world; a moment of even greater significance than his sudden and surprising election by Pharaoh to be his vizier. That event had happened simply to make this possible! Now he saw that, if he could only be restored to a meaningful relationship with his brothers and they themselves could be truly reconciled to the purpose of their election, he could serve his father's God in a unique way and ensure that his family would be preserved to fulfill the call given and the blessing promised to Abraham!

That he had been enabled to see this situation in such a way we have to regard as a marvelous work of the grace of God. Naturally he had been tempted to great bitterness after what some of his brothers had done and others had allowed to be done. How could he even face them again without showing his inner contempt and breaking out into accusation? It is in the light of this temptation that we can interpret the names of the two sons who were born to him at the height of his prosperity. In the given translation of "Manasseh" ("God has made me forget all my hardship and all my father's house"), the use of the word "forget" does not mean that he was helped by God to blot his family out of his memory but rather that he was enabled by the grace of God to blot out all the bitterness against them that tended to defile his memory and all his personal relations with them. He was yearning for a reconciliation with them that would now (to quote the meaning of Ephraim in 41:52) "make fruitful" what he had experienced "in the land of his misfortune." He was beginning even at this stage of his life to grasp the wonder of God's providential working, which he was later to express in unforgettable words (45:7-8): "God sent me before you to preserve for you a remnant on earth, and to keep alive for you many survivors. So it was not you who sent me here, but God." He was certain, too, that God had already begun in the minds and hearts of his brothers in Canaan a work that would prove in the long run to be as powerful and miraculous as any he had inwardly experienced. The dream that he had had in Canaan had come powerfully back to his mind. God was now seeking through him to restore to the whole family of Israel all the faith, pride, hope, and sense of his continual presence that had sustained Abraham, Isaac, and Jacob throughout their lives.

It is with these thoughts in mind that Joseph looked forward to the encounter with his brothers which he was certain God would bring about. God, he believed, was seeking to reconcile them to himself and to the purpose he had called them to fulfill among the nations.

Pastoral Strategy

He saw the task before him as pastoral. He was meant to help them understand God's righteous and loving purpose, in what had happened in himself and in what was happening to them. They must learn to respond with the openness and surrender that would bring about the healing change of heart they so much needed. In the momentary thrill of the re-encounter, Joseph must have felt tempted to reveal himself there and then, to embrace these men as his brothers, to tell the wonderful self-vindicating story of how God had preserved him so that his dream might be fulfilled. But he had cause to be thankful that they showed no sign of recognizing him, and his wisdom held. There were questions that needed answering before he could be sure of his ground. The whole future of God's people would be in danger if he mistakenly preferred the brief satisfaction of an emotional moment or two of reunion before finding his answers. He was certain that his brothers' deepest need was to be reoriented to the God of their fathers for forgiveness and new life. The biggest danger was that some cheap and easy substitute should divert them from what alone was genuine. Who would really profit if he gave them everything the kingdom of Egypt could offer, when at the same time they missed everything the God of their fathers might be seeking to open before them? He believed, therefore, that he could never be justified in revealing himself to his brothers or in offering them his fellowship until he found in them the signs of true repentance.

At first he was inclined to be overanxious and hasty. He accused them of spying because he wanted an excuse to imprison them all while he sent one of them back for Benjamin. By observing them in prison he could make some estimate of how far they had come and how far he could move towards the great day when, as he believed firmly, his dream would be fulfilled. But the conviction came to him that he needn't hurry. God had kept him waiting long in prison before his release. He must be equally patient for the greater work of God that he felt was imminent. There was, moreover, an urgent need for food in Canaan; he must send it back quickly. He decided to detain one of his brothers and wait for God to show him the next step.

We can best understand Joseph's dealing with his brothers if we interpret him as simply seeking to cooperate with what he believed God had already begun and would bring to fruition, completing the healing of his chosen family and restoring his blessing to it. The most adequate language we have today for Joseph's prayer and hope is that God would reconcile them to himself and make them new creatures. Joseph was confident in seeking this because he believed God was already working miraculously to make it happen. We can thus understand his longer-term strategy. He knew he could ensure their personal return if he kept one of them in prison. And as he sent them back with food he tried to ensure that their thoughts would be centered on God. He reminded them of God's intimate knowledge of all our doings, and the ultimate severity of his final judgment on our guilt — death! *"Do this,"* he said to them in prison, *"and you will live, for I fear God; if you are honest men . . . your words will be verified, and you shall not die"* (vv. 18-20). Why should they be worried if there is a God in heaven?

Along with "God" he had already put "Joseph" in their minds. When they were singled out — spoken to roughly, questioned, falsely accused, thrown into prison — he had hoped they would think of what their young brother must have felt that day! Their situation was further shaped to remind them of Joseph when he selected Simeon, had him bound before their eyes in the same way he himself had been bound, and sent them home with a report to give to their father

of one more lost son. "He pleasantly initiates all these actions recip-
rocally which they in despite and earnest had done formerly to him,"
says Joseph Hall quaintly. "He speaks roughly, rejects their persua-
sions, puts them in the hold, and one of them in bonds."

With the thought of God implanted in their minds, and the
word "Joseph" written in all the new circumstances that face them,
conscience continues to work. Their misery helps: "Nothing doth so
powerfully call home the conscience as affliction," continues Bishop
Hall, "neither need there any other art or memory for sin as misery."
Memory indeed began to work, and they began to be troubled. *"They
said to one another, 'In truth we are guilty concerning our brother, in that we
saw the distress of his soul, when he besought us and we would not listen; therefore is this distress come upon us'"* (v. 21, RSV). Though they did not
know it, Joseph who was there present, heard every word of their self-
accusation, and of Reuben's further reproach to them (v. 23). It is
significant that he turned away and wept (v. 24).

Their awakened conscience worked, as it sometimes does, irra-
tionally and in an exaggerated manner. This aspect of its working on
the human mind is described for us well in Leviticus: "I will send
faintness into their hearts in the lands of their enemies; the sound of
a driven leaf shall put them to flight, and they shall flee as one flees
from the sword, and they shall fall when none pursues" (Lev. 26:36;
cf. Deut. 28:65-67). "Our whole life," says Luther, commenting on
this state of mind, "hangs in doubt and uncertainty, full of anguish
and terror at any moment of time." The brothers, he notes, were now
troubled not simply about the sin of which they were the cause, but
"they imagined that there was new guilt in every action and
thought." This is why they were so foolishly alarmed when they
found money in the mouth of one of the sacks. A normal reaction
would have been to be thankful for the kindness of their former
host. But they are dismayed, as if they find in this circumstance a
sign that God is somehow pursuing them: *"'My money has been put
back; here it is in my sack,'"* said one of them, *"and they turned trembling*

one to another, saying, 'What is this that God has done to us?'" (v. 28). Is
God reaching down through the distance they know must separate
him from themselves in their sinfulness, and is he really giving them
signs that he may be about to bring judgment upon them?

Stirrings of New Life

When we watch the brothers after they arrive home, and listen to the
talk, it seems as if God has also begun to reach through to their
minds and hearts in a new and creative way. Their burden of conscience grows heavier. After they have told their father about the
man and the prison, about Simeon and the demand to see Benjamin,
each opens his sack and they observe each man's bundle of money. It
is while they are registering their further dismay that their father in a
moment of bitterness openly accuses them of their crime, speaking
of a betrayal of Simeon. *"You have bereaved me of my children: Joseph is no
more, and Simeon is no more, and now you would take Benjamin; all this has
come upon me"* (v. 36, RSV). They dare not challenge his insinuation
that they are responsible for the disappearance of Joseph, and it is to
their credit that they do not try to do so. Moreover it is a sign of
change that these men who sold Joseph for twenty pieces of silver are
now willing to accept God's lesson that the wrong kind of wealth
even innocently gained, like this cash in their sacks, can become a severe burden to its owner.

During the long passage of time at home described at the beginning of chapter 43, we are meant to notice other signs of new beginnings in the life of the family. They are certainly mere signs, but in view
of what follows we can call them first steps in a life of repentance. The
prophet Ezekiel was at one time given a vision of a valley full of dead
bones, scattered all over, dry with not a trace of life anywhere (Ezek.
37). This represented the state of his nation and his church! He was
told to speak to the bones, to call for the Spirit to come upon them,

61

and eventually the miracle was complete. Flesh came upon the bones and the skeletons; all stood up to become a great living army. Ezekiel's account of the vision gives a wonderful picture of how God, through his Word, can renew his people. As we read it, however, our attention is drawn to the first thing that happened as renewal began: the bones that belonged to each other began to move towards each other. "As I prophesied, there was a noise, and behold, a rattling; and the bones came together, bone to its bone" (Ezek. 37:7). The reviving Word of God drew them together. Joseph's brothers are at last beginning to talk with each other about what matters most in their lives! (cf. 42:21, 28). Previously we saw them looking at each other in silence (42:1). But now they share their feelings much more closely. Is there not here a slight movement towards the openness before each other and before God that takes place as new life comes into their midst? A movement of true compassion towards his father Jacob shows itself first in Reuben, and though he is tragically rebuffed it is taken up by Judah. It is in the new relationship between Judah and his father, however, that a significant breakthrough occurs.

Wiser than Reuben, Judah chooses a better time for a closer approach to Jacob. He finds the opportunity later when the family through Jacob's stubbornness are again facing starvation. He lets hungry Jacob begin the conversation: *"Go buy us a little food"* (43:2). The old man possibly hopes that if they go with only a small order, the Egyptian ruler's pity might make him forget his demand to see Benjamin.

Judah tries to be patient. He points out gently that Jacob's delaying tactics have already done them all damage. Without protest, he allows his father to repeat the accusation that they had been foolish to reveal their home circumstances and to mention Benjamin to the man in Egypt. Judah here is genuinely moved by his father's agony. He wants to be on better relations. He pleads for his father simply to begin personally trusting him: *"I will be surety for him: of my hand you shall require him. If I do not bring him back to you and set him before you, then let me bear the blame for ever"* (v. 9, RSV).

And now for the first time since the days when Joseph used to share his burdens and ask his advice, Jacob opens up in trust to an appeal from another of his children. *"If it must be so"* (v. 11) then let them find the best way of ensuring success and of doing it together!

In this turning of Judah towards Jacob and in the opening up of Jacob to Judah we have a sign to make us rejoice. In everything that follows Judah is in a key position, and the relationship between him and his father will have a decisive effect on the family future. Back at home, the work that Joseph has yet to complete is now beginning; it may be seen as a foretaste of great things to come. Here is a father beginning to find one of the sons he had thought dead. Here is a son initiating a deeper relationship with a father he has never before fully appreciated.

Jacob's Sacrifice

It is now one of the greatest moments in Jacob's life when, under the pressure of such hard and binding circumstances, he yields himself before what he believes to be the grace and power of God. Years before, when he had wrestled with the angel at the ford of the Jabbok (cf. 32:22-32), he had learned that it was in this kind of broken weakness that a man can begin to strive "with God and humans" and prevail. An old man now and more broken than ever, he will yield in hope everything he has into the same divine hands. We must try to understand how great a sacrifice of himself, his plans, and his former desires he is making. Never at any moment during these past years has he faced the fact that he must give up Joseph before God. He has continually felt bitter about his lot, and there has been much darkness and misery around him. But now he faces the issue of Joseph as he faces the issue of Benjamin. Does God want Benjamin? He will have everything! *"Take your brother and arise, go again to the man"* (43:13, RSV). He prays that God may spare him the worst. *"May God*

Almighty grant you mercy before the man, that he may send back your other brother and Benjamin" (v. 14). But he is prepared to yield totally: *"If I am bereaved, I am bereaved"* (v. 14). In the total surrender of himself before God he is surrendering at last to the taking of Joseph too!

Of course there is pressure to make him yield: his sons, their wives, their little ones will starve if he does not. But he is yielding with the free assent of his own will, even under such constraining circumstances; his "Yes" before God is a trusting and willing word of true faith. As a sign of his new openness before God, he sends along with Benjamin the best he can give — a few meager luxury goods left in their store, all the more precious because staples are so short. Let them take *"a little balm and a little honey, gum, resin, pistachio nuts, and almonds"* (v. 11).

With great reverence we can compare him at this moment with Mary the mother of Jesus. When she was greeted by the angel and told she had been chosen by God, could she possibly have said No? And yet she was being asked and she yielded freely — "Behold I am the handmaid of the Lord: let it be to me according to your word" (Luke 1:38). We can come under the most intense pressure to do what God wants, to receive what God gives and to yield what God asks. We can do it either under the constraint of grim necessity, or with glad yielding hearts. God wants our free self-offering, as we go his way and yield to his word. We must not underestimate the significance of this very undramatic act of Jacob. The writer takes time to tell it with some detail in the narrative because it is another important step towards the final outcome of all these events. God has not left it all to one man alone.

CHAPTER 7

The Crisis: Joseph and Judah

Genesis 43:15–44:34

---

43 15 So the men took the present, and they took double the money with them, as well as Benjamin. Then they went on their way down to Egypt, and stood before Joseph.

16 When Joseph saw Benjamin with them, he said to the steward of his house, "Bring the men into the house, and slaughter an animal and make ready, for the men are to dine with me at noon." 17 The man did as Joseph said, and brought the men to Joseph's house. 18 Now the men were afraid because they were brought to Joseph's house, and they said, "It is because of the money, replaced in our sacks, the first time, that we have been brought in, so that he may have an opportunity to fall upon us, to make slaves of us and take our donkeys." 19 So they went up to the steward of Joseph's house and spoke with him at the entrance to the house. 20 "Oh, my lord, we came down the first time to buy food; 21 and when we came to the lodging place we opened our sacks, and there was each one's money in the top of his sack, our money in full weight. So we have brought it back with us. 22 Moreover, we have brought down with us additional money to buy food. We do not know who put our money in our sacks." 23 He replied, "Rest assured, do not be afraid; your God and the God of your father must have put treasure in your sacks for you; I received your money." Then

he brought Simeon out to them. 24 When the steward had brought the men into Joseph's house, and given them water, and they had washed their feet, and when he had given their donkeys fodder, 25 they made the present ready for Joseph's coming at noon, for they had heard that they would dine there.

26 When Joseph came home, they brought him the present that they had carried into the house, and bowed to the ground before him. 27 He inquired about their welfare, and said, "Is your father well, the old man of whom you spoke? Is he still alive?" 28 They said, "Your servant our father is well; he is still alive." And they bowed their heads and did obeisance. 29 Then he looked up and saw his brother Benjamin, his mother's son, and said, "Is this your youngest brother, of whom you spoke to me? God be gracious to you, my son!" 30 With that, Joseph hurried out, because he was overcome with affection for his brother, and he was about to weep. So he went into a private room and wept there. 31 Then he washed his face and came out; and controlling himself he said, "Serve the meal." 32 They served him by himself, and them by themselves, because the Egyptians could not eat with the Hebrews, for that is an abomination to the Egyptians. 33 When they were seated before him, the firstborn according to his birthright and the youngest according to his youth, the men looked at one another in amazement. 34 Portions were taken to them from Joseph's table, but Benjamin's portion was five times as much as any of theirs. So they drank and were merry with him.

44 Then he commanded the steward of his house, "Fill the men's sacks with food, as much as they can carry, and put each man's money in the top of the sack. 2 Put my cup, the silver cup, in the top of the sack of the youngest, with his money for the grain." And he did as Joseph told him. 3 As soon as the morning was light, the men were sent away with their donkeys. 4 When they had gone only a short distance from the city, Joseph said to his steward, "Go, follow after the men; and when you overtake then, say to them, 'Why have you returned evil for good? Why have you stolen my silver cup? 5 Is it not from this cup that my lord drinks? Does he not indeed use it for divination? You have done wrong in doing this.'"

6 When he overtook them, he repeated these words to them. 7 They said to him, "Why does my lord speak such words as these? Far be it from your servants that they should do such a thing! 8 Look, the money that we found at the top of our sacks, we brought back to you from the land of Canaan; why then would we steal silver or gold from your lord's house? 9 Should it be found with any one of your servants, let him die; moreover the rest of us will become my lord's slaves." 10 He said, "Even so; in accordance with your words, let it be; he with whom it is found shall become my slave, but the rest of you shall go free." 11 Then each one quickly lowered his sack to the ground, and each opened his sack. 12 He searched, beginning with the eldest and ending with the youngest; and the cup was found in Benjamin's sack. 13 At this they tore their clothes. Then each one loaded his donkey, and they returned to the city.

14 Judah and his brothers came to Joseph's house while he was still there; and they fell to the ground before him. 15 Joseph said to them, "What deed is this that you have done? Do you not know that one such as I can practice divination?" 16 And Judah said, "What can we say to my lord? How can we clear ourselves? God has found out the guilt of your servants; here we are then, my lord's slaves, both we and also the one in whose possession the cup has been found." 17 But he said, "Far be it from me that I should do so! Only the one in whose possession the cup was found shall be my slave; but as for you, go up in peace to your father."

18 Then Judah stepped up to him, "O my lord, let your servant please speak a word in my lord's ears, and do not be angry with your servant; for you are like Pharaoh himself. 19 My lord asked his servants, saying, 'Have you a father or a brother?' 20 And we said to my lord, 'We have a father, an old man, and a younger brother, the child of his old age. His brother is dead; he alone is left of his mother's children, and his father loves him.' 21 Then you said to your servants,

'Bring him down to me, so that I may set my eyes on him.' 22 We said to my lord, 'The boy cannot leave his father, for if he should leave his father, his father would die.' 23 Then you said to your servants, 'Unless your youngest brother comes down with you, you shall see my face no more.' 24 When we went back to your servant my father we told him the words of my lord. 25 And when our father said, 'Go again, buy us a little food,' 26 we said, 'We cannot go down. Only if our youngest brother goes with us, will we go down; for we cannot see the man's face unless our youngest brother is with us.' 27 Then your servant my father said to us, 'You know that my wife bore me two sons; 28 one left me. And I said, "Surely he has been torn to pieces." And I have never seen him since. 29 If you take this one also from me, and harm comes to him, you will bring down my gray hairs in sorrow to Sheol.' 30 Now therefore, when I come to your servant my father and the boy is not with us, then, as his life is bound up in the boy's life, 31 when he sees that the boy is not with us, he will die; and your servants will bring down the gray hairs of your servant our father with sorrow to Sheol. 32 For your servant became surety for the boy to my father, saying, 'If I do not bring him back to you, then I will bear the blame in the sight of my father all my life.' 33 Now therefore please let your servant remain as a slave to my lord in place of the boy; and let the boy go back with his brothers. 34 For how can I go back to my father if the boy is not with me? I fear to see the suffering that would come upon my father."

Joseph Disturbs Us

As we move in this chapter towards the climax of the story of the treatment Joseph gave his brothers, many of us who have understood and admired what he has so far accomplished have our attitude to him disturbed; indeed, we may find ourselves questioning him as he questions his brothers. For a moment or two he seems insensitive to what has taken place under his very eyes; he prolongs his brothers' agony more than they need. The most severe critics accuse him of playing a cat and mouse game. We too begin to wonder if he still harbors a lingering personal resentment over the suffering his brothers inflicted on him. There is no doubt that the narrator, so sensitive in his handling of all his material, intends to share his own impression of Joseph's failure at the climax of the whole drama. He may be gently showing us that when all the other sheaves bowed down, Joseph's sheaf failed to stand upright.

When he saw them returned with Benjamin, Joseph was confident that the time had come when all these deep and vital questions about their readiness to accept forgiveness and enter into a new life with God should be fully answered. He wanted to be sure they had each dealt with themselves before God and were indeed changed men. He devised a searching test in which Benjamin would stand as his substitute. He would put them all into a situation in which Benjamin's life would be at stake. He would see how they behaved towards their younger brother's plight. His plan was simple and easily executed. He would invite them to a meal. He would have his silver cup lying about. He would have it put in Benjamin's sack. He would have them overtaken and searched on their journey home. He would have Benjamin accused and condemned to slavery. In such a crisis, off their guard, he would see how they reacted.

All the details of the arranged reception contributed to the success of his plan. His welcome contrasts with the first encounter, when he put them in prison: this time he brings them to his house for a banquet. Then he was harsh, now he is almost jovial. But one strange incident deepens their fear: when Joseph seats them at table he seats them in exactly the order of their ages (43:33). But they are put at their ease when they express their fears about the money that had been returned in their sacks. Their money had been received. It must have been their God who had showed them this sign of his favor! (43:23). They are uplifted! The meal is splendid. They become assured that their host means them well. They are plied with wine, *"so they drank and were merry with him"* (43:34). Joseph intends that they should be in this way put off guard. The test will be more effective if the shock is as great as possible. He wants to know exactly how they react when they are natural and free. Therefore after the cup has been smuggled into Benjamin's sack they are sent home in high spirits. How good everything is! They are in favor with important people. Their food is guaranteed. Might it not be possible that from now on even their home life with their father will be happier? Then they are stopped and accused! Not one of them imagines for a moment that any of them could have descended to such a petty and foolish act! They vow they will all become slaves of the man if the cup is found in one sack. They are so much off guard that the idea of a plot does not occur to any of them.

The steward plays his part exactly as Joseph has rehearsed it with him. It will be enough if the man in whose sack is found remains as a slave in Egypt forever! It is by the instruction of Joseph that the search takes time; they leave Benjamin's sack to the last. As one after the other is cleared they become more and more confident — and then they are shattered. *"Then they rent their clothes, and every man loaded his ass, and they returned to the city"* (44:13, RSV). We wish that Joseph himself had been there and had seen them rend their clothes at the time of the cup's discovery! Surely this would have been all the proof he had been looking for; they were indeed different men than they had been. Yet even when they return and bow miserably at his feet for mercy he does everything he can to intensify their fears. He refuses to give them credit for the confused confession of their former guilt, and he exaggerates his awesomeness in their sight by claiming supernatural power. Calvin is one of Joseph's severest critics at this point. Only a forced exposition, he thinks, could possibly find excuses for Joseph's pretense that he is a great magician. Joseph, the reformer believed, here profanes the gift of the Holy Spirit and discharges his duty defectively. "In figuring himself to be a stranger to his brethren he combines many falsehoods in one, and takes advantage of the vulgar opinion that he used augurism."

What is at stake at this juncture is of great importance. It is the way in which Joseph wishes to present himself at the critical moment when he makes himself known. How important it is that he should then be able to say: "It is I, Joseph!" and be able to reveal himself as one who has been longing and praying to be one with them at last in brotherly affection. He surely wants them to be able to live down and forget what is behind, and to be able to join with him in a warm-hearted family circle where each can talk trustfully to the other, sharing the blessing. We can see what now, instead, is beginning to happen. He is stamping an entirely false impression of himself on their minds in an overzealous attempt to ensure their repentance.

Judah Steps In

At this critical point in the story, however, God providentially intervenes and we quickly forget Joseph's temporary lapse. Elijah at his moment of psychological collapse was visited by an angel from heaven (1 Kings 19:5). Paul at a critical moment was comforted by the coming of Titus (2 Cor. 7:6). For Joseph, the ministering angel is his elder brother. For a few most significant moments he takes over against Joseph himself. We begin now to understand more clearly why prominence, here and there in the narrative, has already been given to Judah. He too is being called to leadership among the people of God. God has been working no less lovingly and powerfully with Judah's mind and heart than he has with Joseph's. Judah is now ready and able to minister to his younger brother when he needs a friend at his side. Brother faces brother, though one of them does not know it.

"Then Judah went up to him and said, 'O my lord, let your servant, I pray you, speak a word in my lord's ears, and let not your anger burn against your servant. . . .'" (v. 18, RSV). Joseph's bewildering aloofness is broken down by one of the most moving and eloquent speeches in the whole Bible. We have to remember as we read it that it is uttered not simply as a plea from one man to another. Judah, already a completely transformed man, is simply pouring out the prayer of his heart, turning towards God in a clinging desperate hope that he and his young brother Benjamin — and his father too — may be shown mercy by God, in their otherwise helpless need. He is even more conscious of God now than of the man before him. He is waging a battle for the heart and mercy of God, as he tries at the same time to win the heart and mercy of this strange ruler.

The urgency of his need drives him to boldness in his approach. He feels so helpless that he cannot afford to be cautious even before this awesome and threatening man. He raises himself from his knees (v. 18) to plead with him face to face about those life-and-death issues which, when they are honestly and openly faced, level all humanity. He dares, indeed, to argue with the man before him and to throw much of the responsibility for what has happened on his shoulders. If it had not been for the question that had been asked, and the requests to have Benjamin brought to Egypt, their plight would never have occurred: *"My lord asked. . . . Then you said. . . . Then you said . . ."* (vv. 19-23). He is speaking to God at the same time he is speaking to Joseph, for he is acutely conscious that God — who has continually controlled everything that has so broken and changed him — is personally there listening to every word. And he is speaking in complete solidarity with all his brothers, for he knows that they too have felt God dealing with them as a group. His mercy has been common as their sinfulness was common. They are all of them confused. The majestic, frightening, and strange man seems to stand before them in the place of God. God has reached down into their hearts through what he has said and done to them.

72

The burden of everything Judah said is given in the confession, *"God has found out the guilt of your servants"* (44:16). They have felt compelled to trace everything that has happened to God! They are sure that young Benjamin could never have done it! They do not suspect a plot by their Egyptian host. Their disaster is to them unexplained except by the hand of God! It is he who has been pursuing them and interfering with them these past months. Did he not even put the money in their sacks? It is God who has put the cup where it has been found — a sign of his judgment upon them for their criminal past. They can now be crushed by the accusation of a sin they did not commit because they are aware of the sin they have committed. They are too conscious of God and their own sin to complain or rebel. They can resist no more what they believe to come from God. They are surrendered. They now know that their lives and destiny are in his hands. They are willing to accept his sentence. No punishment can be unjust in the light of what they have done. They are grieved for their innocent brother Benjamin. Their burden is the greater because they seem to have involved him, too, in their guilt and judgment.

As Judah explains the difficulties his request raised with their father and the pledge he himself has made, his prayer tends, finally, to direct itself towards Joseph. Can this man with so much power not see and feel the situation, and therefore understand and yield? He argues while he pleads. Yet while he argues boldly he is at the same time pleading for mercy. He is a suppliant who punctuates the whole petition with the language of abasement, ". . . *let your servant speak . . . your servant . . . my lord asked his servants . . . your servant my father. . . .*" He is concerned only for others. If there is a trace of self-centeredness in what he is requesting it is only because, like his own father, his life is *"bound up with"* (vv. 30-31) the lives of everyone else concerned.

If it pleases God he will himself accept the worst. But he cannot face seeing the worst happen to others whom he loves so much. Can this be what life is for? He is so moved by the tragedy of the situation, and his own passion, that his Spirit-inspired pleading takes on an almost sublime eloquence. *"Now therefore,"* he pleads, *"when I come to your servant my father, and the lad is not with us, then, as his life is bound up with the lad's life, when he sees that the lad is not with us, he will die; and your servants will bring down the gray hairs of your servant our father with sorrow to Sheol. . . . Now therefore let your servant, I pray you, remain instead of the lad as a slave to my lord, and let the lad go back with his brothers. For how can I go back to my father if the lad is not with me? I fear to see the evil that would come upon my father"* (vv. 30-34, RSV).

Luther indeed regarded Judah's whole utterance as a model for all prayer: "It was his purpose to soften Joseph. Indeed nothing is omitted that could move and constrain Joseph's heart. . . . No man could despise a prayer like this." He admired especially Judah's ardor: "I surely could not speak this way and I cannot explain the feeling with which he poured it forth before Joseph. . . . Would that we were able to call upon God with the ardor with which Judah prays before his brother."

Towards Understanding Joseph

Joseph succeeded in what he prayed to God to help him to do. He was instrumental in bringing his whole family and even his father (cf. 49:25-26) back to God. He was at least in part responsible for the conversion of Judah. Since we can now review the whole course of his ministry to his brothers, we are forced to think again as to whether our momentary criticism of him was justified. We must not fail to take note of, and indeed learn from, the witness he steadfastly gave as he tried to serve God.

It helps us to appreciate him if we become clear about the problem he was facing and what was in his mind as he tried to deal with it. After all, he was engaged in the same kind of pastoral work that faces us constantly in our church and family circles today. Jesus used expressive language to describe the power we have at times to represent him and to offer forgiveness. He said to his disciples: "I will give you the keys of the kingdom of heaven, and whatever you bind on earth shall be bound in heaven, and whatever you loose on earth shall be loosed in heaven" (Matt. 16:19). Elsewhere he said, "If you forgive the sins of any, they are forgiven; if you retain the sins of any, they are retained" (John 20:23). Paul speaks of himself as having received a "ministry of reconciliation" (2 Cor. 5:18), and as having been given "the stewardship of God's grace" (Eph. 3:2). Such words, of course, apply directly and personally to those who are called to preach the Word of God, to administer the sacraments and exercise discipline within the church. But in ordinary situations we are all of us at times in Joseph's position. We have to act as preacher, pastor, bishop — as one who is in the place of God — towards others. At times, moreover, God places us within our own family life as peacemakers, to pray for and even maneuver a way for forgiving love to enter where bitterness and hatred have prevailed. Paul wrote to the Galatians: "If a man is caught doing something wrong, my brothers, you who are endowed with the Spirit must set him right again very gently" (Gal. 6:1, NEB) Obviously he is writing to the ordinary members of the whole congregation, and he is reminding them that they *all* have the task of "setting people right" again!

When John Knox in his *Scots Confession* was describing what takes place within us as we find ourselves forgiven, he described it in very practical terms: "We begin," he wrote, "to hate those things which we at first loved, and to love those things we formerly hated." This describes exactly the inward change that Joseph expected God to effect in the thought, attitude, and will of each of his brothers, without the evidence of which he could never have offered them God's forgiveness. He had to find evidence of a radical conversion. To him God was always wonderful in all his ways, and he expected from him a powerful and, indeed, miraculous response to his hopes and prayers.

It would not have been enough that they should have turned towards the light and made progress towards it. He does not think of meeting them in some halfway house and encouraging them to continue. His expectation is that they must have arrived, must have entered the door, crossed the line. He wants evidence that they have come out of darkness into light, out of death into life.

We are forced to ask how much justification we can find in the New Testament for his stance. We believe that Calvin, as usual, puts its teaching with admirable brevity and clarity. "Forgiveness of sins," he wrote, "can never be obtained without repentance." Yet he was careful to add that "repentance is not the cause of forgiveness of sins." We cannot have the one without the other or the other without the one, because both inseparably happen to us when Christ himself in pure grace comes to dwell in us. The New Testament, we believe, allows us more latitude than seemed possible to Joseph and demands of us great patience in our dealings with those around us in the church who accept the Christian faith. "First the stalk, then the head, then the full grain in the head" (Mark 4:28) is the advice given by Jesus in one of his parables. We must not question too searchingly the gradual steps we find taking place within individuals as the Spirit begins his work in them through the Word. It can be a decisive step when somehow hearing his voice they begin to open their lives to his moral influence, denying their desires and accepting as their appointed cross the hardship of the way before them.

Yet Joseph, we believe, was as marvelously near the truth as any prophet or teacher ever became in the movement of the Old Testament towards the New. He can certainly be faulted for being so one-sided. Yet from where he stood it was almost impossible for him to see the other side. We therefore find ourselves wanting to supplement rather than correct the stance he took. His particular concern in his day was to fill with meaning, content, and reality an encounter which, when he first faced its possibility, threatened to become empty. We ourselves, with our gospel of what is sometimes defined as "unconditional grace" — our far too lavish offers of forgiveness without repentance, our far too easy acceptance of each other and of everybody in the name of Christ, "just as we are" — find ourselves trapped too often in the serious fault that Joseph was seeking to avoid.

CHAPTER 8

"I Am Joseph"

Genesis 45:1-15

45 Then Joseph could no longer control himself before all those who stood by him, and he cried out, "Send everyone away from me." So no one stayed with him when Joseph made himself known to his brothers. ² And he wept so loudly that the Egyptians heard it, and the household of Pharaoh heard it. ³ Joseph said to his brothers, "I am Joseph. Is my father still alive?" But his brothers could not answer him, so dismayed were they at his presence.

⁴ Then Joseph said to his brothers, "Come closer to me." And they came closer. He said, "I am your brother, Joseph, whom you sold into Egypt. ⁵ And now do not be distressed, or angry with yourselves, because you sold me here; for God sent me before you to preserve life. ⁶ For the famine has been in the land these two years; and there are five more years in which there will be neither plowing nor harvest. ⁷ God sent me before you to preserve for you a remnant on earth, and to keep alive for you many survivors. ⁸ So it was not you who sent me here, but God; he has made me a father to Pharaoh, and lord of all his house and ruler over all the land of Egypt. ⁹ Hurry and go up to my father and say to him, 'Thus says your son Joseph, God has made me lord of all Egypt; come down to me, do not delay. ¹⁰ You shall settle in the land of Goshen, and you shall be near me, you and your children and chil-

dren's children, as well as your flocks, your herds, and all that you have. ¹¹ I will provide for you there — since there are five more years of famine to come — so that you and your household, and all that you have, will not come to poverty.' ¹² And now your eyes and the eyes of my brother Benjamin see that it is my own mouth that speaks to you. ¹³ You must tell my father how greatly I am honored in Egypt, and all that you have seen. Hurry and bring my father down here." ¹⁴ Then he fell upon his brother Benjamin's neck and wept, while Benjamin wept upon his neck. ¹⁵ And he kissed all his brothers and wept upon them; and after that his brothers talked with him.

The Shedding of Aloofness and Artificiality

Joseph could not fail to recognize the transformation that had taken place. Here was a brother towards whom he had lived with deep suspicion, now addressing him man to man, face to face, with transparent guilelessness, hiding nothing of his sin or his heart. It was the miracle he had been waiting for, the answer to his prayers. In response he felt he had to answer the approach with the same kind of openness and passion. He had to seek to come as close to his brother as his brother had tried to come to him. He had therefore to try to throw off everything that had hindered such fellowship — his aloofness and his doubts. He was so moved that he *"could not control his feelings"* (45:1, NEB). He had to reveal himself: *"I am Joseph. Is my father still alive?"* (v. 3). This cry at this moment was more than a simple announcement of his personal name and identity. It was the announcement that he himself, helped by Judah, had at last been able to find himself again — that he is still the same as he was, years ago, at home. He is the one who came to Dothan that day with good will, and a message from his father. In friendship again towards his brothers, he can share with them the great longing which during the long days of waiting has been a burden on his heart: Is my father well, and will I now really be able to see him again?

If his aloofness was to be laid aside, all artificiality had also to be laid aside. The posing and the acting that he had felt so necessary to ensure and test his brothers' repentance had to cease. He tried, more over, to break the crust of artificiality acquired during his years of life in the Egyptian court. *"He cried, 'Make everyone go out from me.' So no one stayed with him when Joseph made himself known to his brothers"* (v. 1, RSV). There was no longer a place for maintaining pomp and dignity among those who knew that all that matters is rightness with God and true relations with one another. Joseph knew that the symbols of his wealth and earthly greatness were keeping him from the full expression of his heart in its movement towards the truth. For an important moment or two, at least, openness to the Spirit of God forced him to break away from the rigid conventions around him.

We are reminded, as we often are in the Bible, that we too easily acquire and cultivate artificial conventions that keep us distanced from others. Of course we cannot live healthy and moral lives without conventions. Things have to be done decently and in order. Good manners and customs give us protection against bad manners and customs, and against the destructive power of our naked lusts and natural aggressiveness. Even badges and ranks, though superficial, can be part of good manners and customs. We are tempted, however, to over-indulge in artificiality, to hide our real selves and to hide from our real selves. We even try to harness it into the service of the gospel by structuring our church life according to the patterns of the world, and by assuming within its fellowship attitudes and styles that belong to an alien world. Robes and processions can certainly give "decency and order" to our church services. But we are often tempted to overdo it. "Some churches," remarked Sydney Smith, "are dying of dignity."

In the early church they understood why Joseph bade all the Egyptians around him to leave him alone while he *"made himself known to his brothers"* (v. 1). When people then presented themselves and their children for baptism they were asked if they renounced "the world and its pomps." We, too, grieve and hinder the Spirit of God if we fail to understand how the cross of Christ constrains us to "lay in dust life's glory dead." As we watch how Joseph acts in revealing himself to his brothers we find ourselves close to the gospel and close to the ways God deals with us in Christ. No mere message! "God was in Christ reconciling the world to himself" (2 Cor. 5:19). "God shows his love to us" (Rom. 5:8). No more restraint! "When he was yet at a distance, his father saw him and had compassion and ran and embraced him and kissed him" (Luke 15:20).

The Good News about God and Their Future

When he bid them *"come closer"* (v. 4) it was because he felt, as a preacher sometimes feels before his congregation, that even group-distance prevents him from saying adequately the personal word he has for each of them. Joseph knew that each of them had dealt with God about his sin. He knew also that God had dealt with and was dealing with each. What they now needed was the further assurance that he himself, Joseph, was personally longing to go forward with each of them into a true family relationship, in which the whole wretched past could be blotted out: *"I am your brother. . . . Do not be distressed, or angry with yourselves"* (vv. 4-5). It is important that we should notice that the central burden of everything else he said was simply good news about God. He made no attempt to give them pastoral counseling about how to deal with the state of shock or psychological trauma he knew they must each be undergoing.

Nor did he speak at all about himself. In what he said there is not a breath of reproach, and there is no reference to any hurt he had ever felt. Obviously the grace of God given to him through all these waiting years had enabled him to deal powerfully and adequately with all his former resentment, all his self-centered questioning, and all the memory of past injury. He had gradually but effectively gone through an experience similar in effect to that described by the apostle Paul: "I have been crucified with Christ, and it is no longer I who live, but it is Christ who lives in me" (Gal. 2:20). Here, as often in the Old Testament, we have a clear sign that all the sanctifying and liberating experiences made possible through Christ's death and victory were already enjoyed by those who felt his presence and power as they looked towards his coming in the flesh.

Joseph's good news about God was not only that in pure love God cancels the guilt and power of human sin and restores us to fellowship with himself, but that he is so completely in control of all events that he can make what is done with malice serve the purposes of grace. He asked them to look at what God had *done* with their sin! Had he not turned it all into good? The very deed of which they were so ashamed, he now insists three times, God has used, making it his own deed to serve his own purposes: *"God sent me. . . . God sent me. . . . It was not you but God"* (vv. 5, 7, 8). He is trying to turn their dismay into wonder and joy, into thankfulness and devotion, at the thought of what God can do with any form of human defiance.

His good news was not only about God but about their family destiny and future history. God was going to continue to be close to them as a family and to work in their midst in the same powerful way they had just witnessed. He would continue to do wondrous things (cf. Ps. 86:10) in Israel so that their history would be shaped and controlled as that of no other nation as it moved through future ages towards the fulfillment of the promise given to Abraham. They would be a nation so blessed that through them the whole world would be blessed. As they grew in Egypt into a nation and somehow eventually returned to their own land, God was going to retain this same unique and powerful hold on all their affairs. We find here the roots of a quite remarkable insight into Israel's future history, an insight shared by all the succeeding prophets of Israel. Isaiah, for instance, made the point that no matter how fierce the opposition of other nations might be, God would fulfill his purpose for them; he would do even impossible things to deliver them from all that hindered their progress as they struggled to keep their identity (cf. Isa. 49:24-26). Jeremiah suggested that even if the people of Israel became obstinate and refused to surrender to God's will and walk in his ways, God would still keep them in his hands and chastise and discipline them in the way a potter molds the clay of a spoiled vessel until there finally emerges "a new vessel as seemed good to the potter to make it" (Jer. 18:4). Indeed, in one place Jeremiah describes God as powerful and creative enough to make them in his hands "a new creation" (Jer. 31:4).

When Paul in Romans 8:28 quotes Joseph and seeks to elaborate on what this can mean to us today, he is reminding us that we ourselves in Christ are the children of Abraham and heirs of the promises made to him. We are thus to regard ourselves as part of the same movement of salvation history as Joseph and his family and the nation Israel throughout its history. We can apply to ourselves all the great promises that the Old Testament prophets following Joseph claimed for God's elect people. Even when things seem entirely against us, God will be "for us" (Rom. 8:31) with marvelous companionship and strength, and at times with results that seem downright "miraculous."

Indeed, the teaching of Jesus encourages us to expect such providence. Since we are living on the verge of the kingdom of God and are giving its demands priority over all else in life (Mark 1:15; Matt. 6:33), we can expect it now and then to break into our lives in miraculous ways. We can expect to find ourselves able to meet and come through with peace and courage difficulties that previously would have overwhelmed and perhaps embittered us — able, finally, to respond to insult and persecution as Jesus calls us to respond. The as-

tonishing verses in Jesus' teaching about faith that removes mountains, about receiving whatever we ask in prayer "in his name," will
also come home to us — not as impossible ideals, but as powerfully
spoken personal challenges to pray with confidence and urgency for
the removal of harmful obstacles to the true Christian welfare and
happiness of our homes, or to the physical health of friends or loved
ones. We will also tend at times to recognize that in the happenstan-
ces of our daily lives one good thing coinciding with another can be
a special sign that God is working for us in the midst of so much
that is against us (Rom. 8:28).

The Talking

It is mentioned as a significant outcome of all Joseph's pastoral ef-
forts in his self-revelation to his brothers that finally his brothers
"talked with him" (v. 15). A miracle had indeed taken place! The deep
and vicious resentment that had made them so early in their home
life unable to share fellowship with him even by talking and listening had been dealt with, and they had now become natural and at
ease in his presence. How much it can mean in ordinary everyday
life with each other if we are free and open in talking to each other
— conveying goodwill, sympathy, and encouragement, sharing our
visions and observations of the world around and enlarging each
other's experience, sharing our burdens and finding support in
each other as we also listen and are listened to in the midst of the
talk!

We do not doubt that Joseph, in addition, hoped that their sense
of wonder at what had taken place and at the great new possibilities
for their family future opening before them would compel them to
talk especially to each other about God. He may indeed have hoped
that some of them might now want to share with him how God had
dealt with them in these recent months or years. In many of the

psalms, when people felt constrained by God to praise him, they often at the same time wanted to talk about God with those around them as they praised him. "O magnify the Lord with me, and let us exalt his name together" (Ps. 34:3). In the church in the New Testament times, in addition to organizing themselves for common worship, Christians also met with each other in smaller gatherings, from "house to house"; there, as well as praying together, and as one aspect of praying together, they could talk with each other about the great new things they were seeing and hearing and beginning to understand as the Bible passages before them took meaning.

It is our conviction that God means this kind of talking to each other to have an important place in the life of any ongoing church, if it is to have full health and true missionary zeal. Paul no doubt had this aspect of our life together in mind when he wrote to the Ephesians: "I pray that you may have the power to comprehend, *with all the saints,* what is the breadth and length and height and depth, and to know the love of Christ that surpasses knowledge, so that you may be filled with all the fullness of God" (Eph. 3:18-19). The italicized words remind us how helpful talking with each other in small group fellowship can be in enlarging our own vision and deepening our Christian experience (cf. 2 Pet. 3:18). Certainly in our common worship, in hearing the Word and participating in the Lord's Supper, and in our singing and praying together we can have deeply felt fellowship without such talking to each other. Yet it is our belief that Christ is in our midst today seeking to use every means within our community life to enable the blind to see, the deaf to hear, and the dumb to speak (cf. Mark 7:37; Matt. 15:30-31). As he does so, even the ordinary member will at times feel under the same impulsion as inspired the apostles to witness boldly before the Jewish Sanhedrin: "We cannot keep from speaking about what we have seen and heard!" (Acts 4:20).

CHAPTER 9

Jacob Recalled and Renewed

Genesis 45:16–46:30

45 **16** When the report was heard in Pharaoh's house, "Joseph's brothers have come," Pharaoh and his servants were pleased. **17** Pharaoh said to Joseph, "Say to your brothers, 'Do this; load your animals and go back to the land of Canaan. **18** Take your father and your households and come to me, so that I may give you the best of the land of Egypt, and you may enjoy the fat of the land.' **19** You are further charged to say, 'Do this; take wagons from the land of Egypt for your little ones and for your wives, and bring your father, and come. **20** Give no thought to your possessions, for the best of all the land of Egypt is yours.'"

21 The sons of Israel did so. Joseph gave them wagons according to the instructions of Pharaoh, and he gave them provisions for the journey. **22** To each one of them he gave a set of garments; but to Benjamin he gave three hundred pieces of silver and five sets of garments. **23** To his father he sent the following: ten donkeys, loaded with the good things of Egypt, and ten female donkeys loaded with grain, bread, and provision for his father on the journey. **24** Then he sent his brothers on their way, and as they were leaving he said to them, "Do not quarrel along the way." **25** So they went up out of Egypt and came to their father Jacob in the land of Canaan. **26** And they told him, "Joseph is still alive! He is even ruler over the land of Egypt." He was stunned; he could not believe them. ²⁷ But when they told him all the words of Joseph that he had said to them, and when he saw the wagons that Joseph had sent to carry him, the spirit of their father Jacob revived. ²⁸ Israel said, "Enough! My son Joseph is still alive. I must go and see him before I die."

46 When Israel set out on his journey with all that he had and came to Beer-sheba, he offered sacrifices to the God of his father Isaac. ² God spoke to him in visions of the night, and said, "Jacob, Jacob." And he said, "Here I am." ³ Then he said, "I am God, the God of your father; do not be afraid to go down to Egypt, for I will make of you a great nation there. ⁴ I myself will go down with you to Egypt, and I will also bring you up again; and Joseph's own hand shall close your eyes."

⁵ Then Jacob set out from Beer-sheba; and the sons of Israel carried their father Jacob, their little ones, and their wives, in the wagons that Pharaoh had sent to carry him. ⁶ They also took their livestock and the goods that they had acquired in the land of Canaan, and they came into Egypt, Jacob and all his offspring with him, ⁷ his sons' sons with him, his daughters, and his sons' daughters; all his offspring he brought with him into Egypt.

⁸ Now these are the names of the Israelites, Jacob and his offspring, who came into Egypt. Reuben, Jacob's first-born, ⁹ and the children of Reuben: Hanoch, Pallu, Hezron, and Carmi. ¹⁰ The children of Simeon: Jemuel, Jamin, Obad, Jachin, Zohar, and Shaul, the son of a Canaanite woman. ¹¹ The children of Levi: Girshon, Kohath, and Meran. ¹² The children of Judah: Er, Onan, Shelah, Perez, and Zerah (but Er and Onan died in the land of Canaan); and the children of Perez were Hezron and Hamul. ¹³ The children of Isaachar: Tola, Puvah, Jashub, and Shimron. ¹⁴ The children of Zebulun: Sered, Elon, and Jahleel. ¹⁵ (These are the sons of Leah, whom she bore to Jacob in Paddan-aram, together with his daughter Dinah; in all his sons and his daughters numbered thirty-three). ¹⁶ The children of Gad: Ziphion, Haggi, Shuni, Ezbon, Eri, Arodi, and Areli. ¹⁷ The children of

Asher: Imnah, Ishvah, Ishvi, Beriah, and their sister Serah. The children of Beriah: Heber and Malchiel 18 (these are the children of Zilpah, whom Laban gave to his daughter Leah; and these she bore to Jacob — sixteen persons). 19 The children of Jacob's wife Rachel: Joseph and Benjamin. 20 To Joseph in the land of Egypt were born Manasseh and Ephraim, whom Asenath daughter of Potiphera, priest of On, bore to him. 21 The children of Benjamin: Bela, Becher, Ashbel, Gera, Naaman, Ehi, Rosh, Muppim, Huppim, and Ard 22 (these are the children of Rachel, who were born to Jacob — fourteen persons in all). 23 The children of Dan: Hashum. 24 The children of Naphtali: Jahzeel, Guni, Jezer, and Shillem 25 (these are the children of Bilhah, whom Laban gave to his daughter Rachel, and these she bore to Jacob — seven persons in all). 26 All the persons belonging to Jacob who came into Egypt, who were his own offspring, not including the wives of his sons, were sixty-six persons in all. 27 The children of Joseph, who were born to him in Egypt, were two; all the persons of the house of Jacob who came into Egypt were seventy.

28 Israel sent Judah ahead to Joseph to lead the way before him into Goshen. When they came to the land of Goshen, 29 Joseph made ready his chariot and went up to meet his father Israel in Goshen. He presented himself to him, fell on his neck, and wept on his neck a good while. 30 Israel said to Joseph, "I can die now, having seen for myself that you are still alive."

A New Era in Israel's History

It has now become obvious what God's purpose has been in all that has happened. He has chosen Egypt to provide the environment for the next crucial stage in the growing life of Israel as a nation. He has chosen to locate them in Egypt for this stage in their history, because here in Goshen, a largely vacant province, they could live in real apartness, sheltered from the pagan influence that had been so hard to resist in Canaan. Here in Goshen as they grew in numbers God would create — through the vision and inspiration of their leaders and elders — the beginnings of the unique moral and religious tradition that would eventually enable them to give the whole alien world around them a clear witness to the truth and power of the living God.

It is remarkable that Pharaoh himself was inspired to take the initiative in deciding this move. While Joseph was busy making it up to his brothers behind closed doors, and had no time to communicate with Pharaoh, the news of his brothers' arrival had reached the palace; Pharaoh himself sent orders to Joseph for all of it to happen! Time after time in Israel's history, great earthly rulers are inspired to be friends rather than persecutors of God's people. Later on God will impel Cyrus of Persia to deliver the impotent and disabled nation from their captivity in Babylon and ensure their return to their own land (cf. Isa. 45). And in Nehemiah's account, Artaxerxes, one of Cyrus's successors, was moved to give help in rebuilding the walls of Jerusalem at a critical time because the "gracious hand of God" inspired him when Nehemiah pled for the king's help (cf. Neh. 2:1-8). Today's church need never be ashamed to accept help or even privilege.

Joseph lost no time when he heard Pharaoh's message. His acceptance of these promises and privileges should be an example to us: we should take God at his word and live up to what he challenges us to enjoy and become. The caravans Joseph prepares were as splendid as Egypt could muster, and to save his brothers from looking impoverished in the midst of Egyptian splendor he gave them each new clothes to fit their new status and surroundings. When it came to Benjamin he could not help a touch of favoritism — after all, the boy had suffered hours of torment under wrong accusation and threat of a life of slavery.

We interpret Joseph's parting remark, *"Do not quarrel along the way"* (v. 24), as a healthy sign that even when he had cause to marvel and be grateful for the transformation God had so far worked in the life of his family he was shrewd enough not to take everything for granted. Attitudes and outlook can be suddenly and genuinely changed when conversion occurs, but there remain large areas of life where the gradually transforming work of God needs time to have full possession of us. We will later discover how Reuben and Simeon eventually found the way too hard to follow. Joseph knew that as his brothers tried to comply with his arrangements, the old rivalries about place and precedence could still arise among them. Paul, in the New Testament, brings us down to earth in much the same way. "Let us not become conceited," he wrote, "competing against one another, envying one another" (Gal. 5:26). Our Lord himself recognized that within the church, even in the face of God's lavish grace, we can still compare ourselves to others and hold back effort (Matt. 20:10ff.). No matter how sanctified we think we have become, we need to keep in mind that we ourselves are still very human.

The Renewal of Jacob — The Good News and the Wagons

In his work on Joseph to which we have already referred (p. 16), as he concludes his continuous discussion of the text, Claus Westermann points out that, apart from a short passage (Gen. 50:15-21), most of the remaining stories are more about the fortunes and future of Jacob and his family than about Joseph. Once the great news from Joseph arrives in Canaan along with the wagons, it is Jacob who is now expected to take over the leadership. Joseph, in the hands of God, has completed the incidental task God gave him within the life of the last of the great patriarchs.

The fact that Jacob was at first *"stunned"* and *"could not believe them"* (v. 26) when he heard the news about Joseph shows us how the

90

concealed lie about the bloodstained coat had gradually worked into all his familial relations. He had begun to sense the surrounding insincerity, there and then, as they *"rose up to comfort him"* (37:35), and he had gradually become withdrawn, suspicious of the underlying deceit even when his sons tried to engage him in family fellowship. When they came within the house and he heard from *"them"* the blunt unbelievable facts, his habitual suspicion prevailed. As they went on with the news, however, he found himself listening to the kind of word about God that he knew could only have come from Joseph. He remembered his talks with the boy when Joseph was the only one with whom he could have fellowship. What he was now listening to was true; what he had been told must have happened. God had indeed come into the midst of his family to redeem it from tragedy and evil, to redeem it for himself. The news began to come home to him powerfully as a Word of God that began to renew his faith.

We are meant to notice that it was also the sight of the wagons, when Jacob went outside the house, that so thrilled him: his *"spirit . . . revived"* (v. 27). God knew how low he had sunk in his depression, how great a struggle it would be for his faith to recover simply by hearing a report, however good, and he had furnished visible proof along with the news. God still understands and treats us at times as he did Jacob. Of course it is by hearing the Word that we are able to believe, and able to pass from death to life (John 5:24). "Faith comes from what is heard" (Rom. 10:17), and we are meant to live and walk continually by such faith, rather than by sight (2 Cor. 5:7). But for us too, there are occasions when perhaps to see us through times of special trouble or to encourage us when we tend to depression, God may give us signs, special coincidences, for example, that we recognize as his particular work, as noticeable answers to our prayers. And many of us are drawn to be present at celebrations of the Lord's Supper for similar reasons: as we receive the bread and wine we are assured with the certainty of sight and touch as well as through our hearing that Christ is ours, that we belong to him.

The Vision

Though his sons had eventually to carry him (Gen. 46:5) and he relied on their help (Judah is especially mentioned), it was only through Jacob's decision and constant leadership that this family migration could possibly have taken place. It was by his watchful memory that no one was missed and by his pressure and persuasion that the resistance of those who felt themselves on the fringe and did not want to change was overcome. He alone at the center of things could hold everyone together and check the naturally divisive forces.

When Jacob had had time to think over his decision — so easy to make after hearing the great news — he began to have doubts, especially over one nagging question. All his days he had interpreted God's Word to Abraham as a command to settle down forever in Canaan. Had not Isaac his father taught him this from his boyhood? Might it not be that Joseph had made a tragic mistake in his new interpretation of family affairs? Moreover, there was the natural question about his own ability to keep up the pace and meet the future — after such a serious and prolonged lapse into weakness and failure. What if he had now made another of his too many mistakes?

It was because he was so troubled that on his way south he went to offer sacrifice at one of his father's altars at Beersheba (cf. Gen. 26:23-25) — a sacred place where God in those days had promised to meet with those who came with surrender and faith. He went there hoping for guidance and encouragement, and God did not disappoint him. *"In visions of the night"* (46:2) he heard his name called — the old name Jacob, which he was by now meant to have outlived. It was used to convey a hint of reproach: God knew how far he had lapsed over these past years! Yet in the tone of what was said there was friendliness and trust. Even in Egypt, God would make of him and his family a great nation. Moreover, a promise that had been given him as a boy at Bethel (cf. Gen. 28:15), which time and again had brought him encouragement and strength, was repeated with fresh divine sanction. God would be with him wherever he went, and would bring him back to his homeland in peace. The word of promise closed, marvelously, with a delicate personal touch: *"and Joseph's own hand shall close your eyes"* (46:4).

The Passenger List

The long list of the passengers reminds us that these particular individuals lived in that place at that time and went together on this particular journey. It is a healthy reminder that what we have been reading should be seen as an account of actual historical events. We are too apt to read the story of Joseph and his brothers as if it were simply a good story. God can certainly speak through "stories"; the Old Testament has many of them, and they yield God's intended message when they are read and interpreted as such. The "story of Joseph," even as a story, teaches us many important theological and practical lessons. But here, as in most of the Bible, God is speaking through actual happenings in history. We can hear and understand adequately what God is seeking to say to us through this narrative only when we accept it as a trustworthy account of an important early development in the history of the people of Israel. Only by accepting it this way can we explain its full relevance to the rest of the Bible, and to our present-day situation in Christ.

When we interpret the Scriptures we should always keep in mind that God not only teaches us through history; he also reveals himself through the happenings in the special history of Israel recorded in the Bible. Much of what happens in world history seems chaotic and meaningless. But as we carefully study and seek to grasp what is presented to us about God's doings even in the Old Testament, we discover the kind of person he is in himself. We discover what he rewards and what he punishes, what he loves and what he hates, how faithful he is in keeping his promises, how serious are his demands, how wonderful his forgiving love. Moreover, all of this is preliminary to what is even more amazing and divine — that in Jesus Christ, through his incarnation and the coming of the Spirit, God actually puts himself into history so that we can both know what he is like and encounter him where we are.

In the list, each one is named. Again we are pointed to New Testament truths still relevant to our church and personal life today. Our Good Shepherd calls us each by name! (John 10). We are meant to discover here an early sign of what comes to fuller expression in the promise addressed, pointedly and literally, to each person of the whole community: "Do not fear, for I have redeemed thee; I have called thee by thy name, thou art mine" (Isa. 43; the KJV with its "thee" instead of "you" retains accurately the second person singular of the original Hebrew).

"Now I Can Die"

As Jacob embraced Joseph and his son *"wept on his neck a good while"* he gave expression to his exultation and joy, in words that are worth pausing over: *"Now let me die, since I have seen your face and know that you are still alive"* (v. 30, RSV). He felt he could not ask more from God. His grief has been fully assuaged. His broken heart has been healed. The nightmare years of trial over Joseph's loss had caused him deep questioning over everything he had lived and toiled for. Finally and from now on he is certain that God, not evil, is going to have the last word in his life. He can now look forward fearlessly to the future. His confidence arises, not out of his own inner feelings of personal satisfaction or attainment. He remains the same Jacob! His joy is full, not because it is now well with himself, but because, in spite of himself, it is now well with Joseph — with his family and with God's promises. He is so full of the joy of this rediscovery that he feels there is nothing more he can ask of God's grace. He feels, indeed, that he is no longer needed. The cause has found new leaders; their future is firmly in the hands of God.

We feel justified in finding, in this saying of Jacob, also a note of confidence about his own personal lot after death. When his faith in God was at its low ebb he had certainly at times given way to contemporary notions about a gloomy realm of "Sheol" to which the soul went down (37:35), possibly with sorrow (42:38). From now on, as he nears his own death, such thoughts and fears of "Sheol" have faded. When he is blessing his sons, he will be able to say, "I await your salvation" (49:18). We are reminded here that Jesus accepted as proof of a blessed afterlife for all who share Jacob's faith, the fact that time and again, long after Jacob had died, God spoke of him in the present tense. "He is God not of the dead but of the living" (cf. Mark 12:27).

It is not difficult at this point to move from Jacob in the Old Testament to Simeon in the New. He himself had been like Jacob. He had lived as one "righteous and devout." He had spent his days "looking for the consolation of Israel" (Luke 2:25). He had been inspired by promises and hopes about the people of God, and the coming Messiah from God. These promises had sustained him and kept him in fellowship with God all his days, but had never been fulfilled. When his strength was failing, the Holy Spirit visited him, kindling the old desires to a new intensity and bringing fresh expectancy. Then came the great moment when he saw the Christ child in the temple and took him in his arms and praised God and said,

"Master, now you are dismissing your servant in peace
  according to your word;
for my eyes have seen your salvation."

(Luke 2:28-30)

CHAPTER 10

The Settlement in Egypt: Sidelights on Joseph and Jacob

Genesis 46:31–47:27

46 31 Joseph said to his brothers and to his father's household, "I will go up and tell Pharaoh, and will say to him, 'My brothers and my father's household, who were in the land of Canaan, have come to me.

32 The men are shepherds, for they have been keepers of livestock; and they have brought their flocks, and their herds, and all that they have.' 33 When Pharaoh calls you, and says, 'What is your occupation?' 34 you shall say, 'Your servants have been keepers of livestock from our youth even until now, both we and our ancestors' — in order that you may settle in the land of Goshen, because all shepherds are an abomination to the Egyptians."

47 So Joseph went and told Pharaoh, "My father and my brothers, with their flocks and herds and all that they possess, have come from the land of Canaan; they are now in the land of Goshen." 2 From among his brothers he took five men and presented them to Pharaoh. 3 Pharaoh said to his brothers, "What is your occupation?" And they said to Pharaoh, "Your servants are shepherds, as our ancestors were." 4 They said to Pharaoh, "We have come to reside as aliens in the land; for there is no pasture for your servants' flocks because the famine is severe in the land of Canaan. Now, we ask you, let your servants settle in the land of Goshen." 5 Then Pharaoh said to Joseph, "Your father and your brothers have come to you. 6 The land of Egypt is before you; settle your father and your brothers in the best part of the land; let them live in the land of Goshen; and if you know that there are capable men among them, put them in charge of my livestock."

7 Then Joseph brought in his father Jacob, and presented him before Pharaoh, and Jacob blessed Pharaoh. 8 Pharaoh said to Jacob, "How many are the years of your life?" 9 Jacob said to Pharaoh, "The years of my earthly sojourn are one hundred and thirty; few and hard have been the years of my life. They do not compare with the years of the life of my ancestors during their long sojourn." 10 Then Jacob blessed Pharaoh, and went out from the presence of Pharaoh. 11 Joseph settled his father and his brothers, and granted them a holding in the land of Egypt, in the best part of the land, in the land of Rameses, as Pharaoh had instructed. 12 And Joseph provided his father, his brothers, and all his father's household with food, according to the number of their dependents.

13 Now there was no food in all the land, for the famine was very severe. The land of Egypt and the land of Canaan languished because of the famine. 14 Joseph collected all the money to be found in the land of Egypt and in the land of Canaan, in exchange for the grain that they bought; and Joseph brought the money into Pharaoh's house. 15 When the money from the land of Egypt and from the land of Canaan was spent, all the Egyptians came to Joseph, and said, "Give us food! Why should we die before your eyes? For our money is gone." 16 And Joseph answered, "Give me your livestock, and I will give you food in exchange for your livestock, if your money is gone." 17 So they brought their livestock to Joseph; and Joseph gave them food in exchange for the horses, the flocks, the herds, and the donkeys. That year he supplied them with food in exchange for all their livestock. 18 When that year was ended, they came to him the following year, and said to him, "We cannot hide from my lord that our money is all spent, and the herds of cattle are my lord's. There is nothing left in the sight of my

lord but our bodies and our lands. ¹⁹ Shall we die before your eyes, both we and our land? Buy us and our land in exchange for food. We with our land will become slaves to Pharaoh; just give us seed, so that we may live and not die, and that the land may not become desolate."

²⁰ So Joseph bought all the land of Egypt for Pharaoh. All the Egyptians sold their fields, because the famine was severe upon them; and the land became Pharaoh's. ²¹ As for the people, he made slaves of them from one end of Egypt to the other. ²² Only the land of the priests he did not buy; for the priests had a fixed allowance from Pharaoh, and lived on the allowance that Pharaoh gave them; therefore they did not sell their land. ²³ Then Joseph said to the people, "Now that I have this day bought you and your land for Pharaoh, here is seed for you; sow the land. ²⁴ And at the harvests you shall give one-fifth to Pharaoh, and four-fifths shall be your own, as seed for the field and as food for yourselves and your households, and as food for your little ones." ²⁵ They said, "You have saved our lives; may it please my lord, we will be slaves to Pharaoh." ²⁶ So Joseph made it a statute concerning the land of Egypt, and it stands to this day, that Pharaoh should have the fifth. The land of the priests alone did not become Pharaoh's.

²⁷ Thus Israel settled in the land of Egypt, in the region of Goshen; and they gained possessions in it, and were fruitful and multiplied exceedingly.

Joseph — Wisdom and Tact

The last verse of the passage under review sums up the theme of the whole of it: *"Thus Israel settled in Egypt, in the region of Goshen; and they gained possessions in it, and were fruitful"* (v. 27).

It had always been the conviction of Abraham and his descendants that they were meant ultimately by God to take over the whole land of Canaan as their own native possession, and maintain there for centuries to come their natural identity during the rise and fall of many surrounding empires and cultures. Yet it was now obvious that they could not have developed according to God's purposes if they remained there at this particular time in their history. The loose behavior of Judah, the compromises that Jacob himself had tolerated as he lost control of his family, the rape of Dinah and its disastrous results had proved decisively that the paganism of Canaan was so enticing, and the strength of the natural Baal religions so strong, that they could not possibly have developed in the midst of it the kind of morality reflected in the Ten Commandments, or the conception of a God who was entirely above sex and abhorred its influence in the stimulation of worship.

What we have to understand about the people of Israel at this time is that by nature they were just like us, easily prone to falsehood and distortion in all matters of morality and religious thought (cf. Gen. 6:5; Rom. 1:21), prone to seek satisfaction in the "desire of the flesh, the desire of the eyes and the pride in riches," rather than in doing the will of God (1 John 2:16-17). What they needed at this stage in their development was to find a place where, apart from all the falsehoods of the surrounding world, they could continue to hear, learn, absorb, and practice the renewing and cleansing word that had come to them recently and powerfully through Joseph, and would no doubt continue to come through other chosen leaders, teachers, and prophets as their community life developed in its apartness. Joseph realized, even before Pharaoh suggested his family's immigration, that the province of Goshen would be the ideal place for their new and temporary settlement. It was much better than anything along the Nile. It was borderland, towards Canaan, not densely populated as elsewhere in Egypt. Its relative seclusion would nourish the distinctive aspects of their religion and culture which, Joseph knew, would tend to mark them as "peculiar." If they mixed too closely with certain elements of the population, the more "cultured" Egyptian neighbors would tend to despise them as uncouth. In Goshen they would probably be left to themselves. Their apartness would prevent religious clash with the ambient culture. In new surroundings they would have leisure to think again about their traditions and their past ways; they could develop their customs, thought, and ethos without contamination by the paganism around them. In a few generations the promises and the laws of life in the covenant God had entrusted to them would be redefined for them by a leader like Moses. Goshen was a fertile area, a much easier land than Canaan, and ideal for pasturing flocks — an occupation normally despised by Egyptians, but followed with pride and a sense of meaning by the sons of Israel.

The account of how Joseph introduced his brothers to Pharaoh (vv. 1-6) brings out his tactfulness in finally obtaining the ruler's consent for their settlement. Although he took nothing for granted, he avoided direct pressure on the monarch. He carefully selected which of his brothers should be presented to Pharaoh. He had Goshen mentioned in a petition that stressed the lowly origin and limited occupation of the sons of Israel (v. 4). They are shepherds; they will be happier if they are kept apart! Would not a fringe province like Goshen provide the most suitable surroundings for men with such simple needs? It is a sign of Joseph's extraordinary influence on Pharaoh that he is told not only to select which part of the province would best suit his purpose, but is also empowered to give his people responsibility with the royal cattle and some measure of self-administration.

Jacob — His Suffering and Its Relevance

It had to come — the meeting between Jacob and Pharaoh. All the questions of where his family should live and what they should do

100

would have been settled. Jacob was therefore under no pressure to defer formally to Pharaoh or to seek any favor from him; the way was clear to express himself freely. What happened was spontaneous. Un-awed by the splendor and strangeness of everything around him, Jacob immediately broke the silence by pronouncing a blessing on Pharaoh; he blessed him in greeting, and he blessed him again in parting from him.

We believe the utterance of his blessing is the giving of a sign — the witness of his faith in the promise of God that Abraham and his descendants will become a blessing to *all* nations. In uttering the benediction Jacob is acting symbolically as leader of the people of God. He is declaring that his family's destiny is to bring light and salvation from God to others. He wants Pharaoh to know that in giving hospitality, protection, and nourishment to his people he will now be open to receive through them from God such light, liberty, and life as can be found nowhere else on earth. We believe also that for Jacob on this particular occasion the utterance of the blessing was also the spontaneous expression of an inward upsurge of good will towards those to whom it was spoken. Jacob had at this stage of his life been so renewed and blessed by the Word of God, which had so powerfully reached him with healing and renewal in the depth of his suffering, that he genuinely felt he could confer real benefit on those to whom his "God bless you" was directed.

It is our belief too that this inward sense of blessedness can help us understand Jacob's unexpected and memorable reply to Pharaoh's question, "How old are you?" Suddenly reviewing his life, he answered: *"The years of my earthly sojourn are one hundred and thirty; few and hard have been the years of my life. They do not compare with the years of the life of my ancestors during their long sojourn"* (vv 8-9).

He had always felt about his life, especially when he compared it with those of Isaac and Abraham, that God had taken from him a heavier than usual toll of ordinary human suffering. But he had come to realize that he was able, more than his father had been, to bless people; and the blessing he gave was all the more relevant because he himself had probed so widely and deeply the sorrows and frustrations that can mar human fulfillment and happiness. Jacob had discovered the elementary truth brought out time and again in the Old and New Testaments: that suffering, as an aspect of God's gracious providence in our lives, can enable us to become a means of blessing to others.

In the book of Genesis we are told more about Jacob than Abraham and Isaac put together, and in what we are told he is always either getting into personal trouble, facing personal trouble, or getting out of it. Moreover, the troubles that God has to see him through are in no way heroic or adventurous or, indeed, humanly exalting. His sufferings are as mundane and ordinary as our own. We find him, for instance, caught up in typical family squabbles as a boy, then driven out at an early age. He is conned into unfair and unsuitable employment, and forced into a binding and loveless marriage whose consequences dogged him all his days. The real thing, his marriage to Rachel, was tragically cut short by bereavement. Repeatedly cheated (the deceiver was himself so often deceived!), he courts danger and trouble by paying people back in their own coin, making things worse for himself by his own foolish reactions and mistakes. Here is the man God treats as if he were the most important person in the world! His troubles, of course, are much like our own — troubles we should seek to triumph over by the power of Christ!

Joseph — Misdirected Zeal

We are perhaps perplexed that during the last few years of the prevailing famine, when the poor in Egypt were so desperately suffering from hunger, Joseph deliberately brought the whole population into complete subjection to Pharaoh. He forced the common people to give all their wealth and land to the state, he made them pledge a fifth of their meager income as an annual tax, and he put Pharaoh in a position of absolute power. He created a system in which gross inequality between rulers and ruled would be perpetuated, and he showed no trace of perplexity over the social or practical implications of his actions, or of sympathy for the deepening wretchedness of the common people.

This is the third time in the narrative that Joseph's behavior is open to criticism. So far we have been able to find excuses. We did not repeat the accusations of priggishness, tale-bearing, and self-centeredness that many commentators make of his early conduct at home, because we realize that a deep and sudden religious experience, such as Joseph's, can make it difficult to readjust to the expected patterns of normal life. We have also justified his lapse in sensitivity at the climax of his dealings with his brothers. But in this final case we are forced to join in the censure.

We reject the excuse that in those days the Middle East lacked a developed sense or desire for the rights of individuals, or the sense of social justice characteristic of the later prophets of Israel. Joseph's fault here was simply that he acted harshly and without pity in the face of massive human misery. Of course there is the possible view that God, through Joseph, was deliberately creating in Egypt a tradition of despotism, so that when Israel was ready to return to Canaan there would be a tyrannous Pharaoh who would provoke the plagues and create the dramatic background for the spectacular deliverance from slavery — thus marking the Exodus as the most memorable and instructive of all Old Testament miracles. But even if there is truth in this view it does not excuse Joseph's callous behavior. We believe that if Joseph at the climax of his rule in Egypt had remained as sensitive to God's guidance as he had been during the days of his own suffering and his deep concern over his brothers, he would have acted differently. We have to regard Joseph's attitude and behavior here as a failure to maintain — at the heart of all he did — the depth of his former love for God himself. We have to believe that he was led astray into an uncritical servility towards Pharaoh, making him heedless of others. He was infected by the corruption that so often mars those who wield great power and continually want more power, thus losing the common touch.

It was at the apex of Joseph's career, when he felt perhaps he could now rest on his laurels, that he fell so badly. In this he reminds us of David. After years of struggle David felt he no longer needed to go out to battle; and at home in Jerusalem, "walking on the roof of his house, he saw a woman bathing" (2 Sam. 11:2). The consequences of his fall were bitter. We too often apply the New Testament warnings to be on guard against temptation only where we are assailed by hard circumstances. We need to remember that even when we have fought the good fight and imagine ourselves successful we can be in great danger. Paul, when he reminds us to take up the whole armor of God, also reminds us that when we "have done everything" we should be especially concerned "to stand firm" (Eph. 6:13).

Joseph's attitude in this matter, and his failure to maintain his strong personal love for God, raises challenging questions about both our personal and our church life. Because Joseph lacked, at this stage of his life, the stability of a sustained personal devotion to God, and because he no longer felt the urgency of keeping his family together in the service of God, he easily allowed himself to be caught up zealously in the service of Pharaoh. He allowed this to happen without realizing that he was yielding to serious temptation. It can happen in our lives too. When our vision of what Christ died for grows blurred or distorted — when we close our ears or eyes to the pressing needs around us — our energy and devotion can too readily be taken up by second-best concerns, and sometimes pathetically misdirected. We become shortsighted in our Christian practice; we concentrate on too narrow a field of concern. We need to continually examine ourselves as to whether we, like Joseph, are being caught up uncritically in the same kind of misplaced zeal.

CHAPTER 11

The Blessing of Ephraim and Manasseh

Genesis 47:28–48:22

47 28 Jacob lived in the land of Egypt seventeen years; so the days of Jacob, the years of his life, were one hundred and forty-seven years.

29 When the time of Israel's death drew near, he called his son Joseph and said to him, "If I have found favor with you, put your hand under my thigh and promise to deal loyally and truly with me. Do not bury me in Egypt. 30 When I lie down with my ancestors, carry me out of Egypt and bury me in their burial place." He answered, "I will do as you have said." 31 And he said, "Swear to me"; and he swore to him. Then Israel bowed himself on the head of the bed.

48 After this Joseph was told, "Your father is ill." So he took with him his two sons, Manasseh and Ephraim. 2 When Jacob was told, "Your son Joseph has come to you," he summoned his strength and sat up in bed. 3 And Jacob said to Joseph, "God Almighty appeared to me at Luz in the land of Canaan, and he blessed me, 4 and said to me, 'I am going to make you fruitful and increase your numbers; I will make of you a company of peoples, and will give this land to your offspring after you for a perpetual holding.' 5 Therefore your two sons, who were born to you in the land of Egypt before I came to you in Egypt, are now mine; Ephraim and Manasseh shall be mine, just as Reuben and Simeon are. 6 As for the offspring born to you after them, they shall be

105

yours. They shall be recorded under the names of their brothers with regard to their inheritance. ⁷ For when I came from Paddan, Rachel, alas, died in the land of Canaan on the way, while there was still some distance to go to Ephrath; and I buried her there on the way to Ephrath (that is, Bethlehem)."

⁸ When Israel saw Joseph's sons, he said, "Who are these?" ⁹ Joseph said to his father, "They are my sons, whom God has given me here." And he said, "Bring them to me, please, that I may bless them." ¹⁰ Now the eyes of Israel were dim with age, and he could not see well. So Joseph brought them near him; and he kissed them and embraced them. ¹¹ Israel said to Joseph, "I did not expect to see your face; and here God has let me see your children also." ¹² Then Joseph removed them from his father's knees, and he bowed himself with his face to the earth. ¹³ Joseph took them both, Ephraim in his right hand toward Israel's left, and Manasseh in his left hand toward Israel's right hand, and brought them near him. ¹⁴ But Israel stretched out his right hand and laid it on the head of Ephraim, who was the younger, and his left hand on the head of Manasseh, crossing his hands, for Manasseh was the firstborn. ¹⁵ He blessed Joseph, and said,

> "The God before whom my ancestors
>   Abraham and Isaac walked,
>   the God who has been my shepherd all my life to this day,
> ¹⁶ the angel who has redeemed me from all evil, bless the boys;
>   and in them let my name be perpetuated,
>   and the name of my ancestors Abraham and Isaac;
>   and let them grow into a multitude on the earth."

¹⁷ When Joseph saw that his father laid his right hand on the head of Ephraim, it displeased him; so he took his father's hand, to remove it from Ephraim's head to Manasseh's head. ¹⁸ Joseph said to his father, "Not so, my father! Since this one is the firstborn, put your right hand on his head." ¹⁹ But his father refused, and said, "I know, my son,

I know; he also shall become a people, and he also shall be great. Nevertheless his younger brother shall be greater than he, and his offspring shall become a multitude of nations." [20] So he blessed them that day, saying,

> "By you Israel will invoke blessings, saying,
> 'God make you like Ephraim and like Manasseh.'"

So he put Ephraim ahead of Manasseh.

[21] Then Israel said to Joseph, "I am about to die, but God will be with you and will bring you again to the land of your ancestors. [22] I now give to you one portion more than to your brothers, the portion that I took from the hand of the Amorites with my sword and with my bow."

Joseph — A Challenge to Personal Recommitment

In this and the next chapter of Genesis the chief concern of the writer is to show us how Jacob, full of inner peace about God and the future of his family, was enabled finally and memorably to bless each of his children. We should first take note, however, of what the narrative tells us about Joseph. It proves decisively that the lapse we have regretted because of its political and personal implications was merely that — a lapse. Even in the midst of all his earthly power, Joseph, in the long run, did not forget the chief aim and purpose of his career as God had designed it: to devote himself whole-heartedly to the service of God's people, and to care first for their welfare. The Epistle to the Hebrews claims that at the very end of his life he was wholly devoted to this one great cause. "By faith Joseph at the end of his life made mention of the exodus of the Israelites" (Heb. 11:22).

As whole-heartedly as he had served the king of Egypt, he had tried always to make his two sons proud of their membership in the chosen people of God. When he heard that his father was ill he felt the time had come to ensure where their future lot would be finally cast. He hurried with them to the deathbed, so that his father might bless them both. The two sons themselves may have helped their father decide; they were certainly old enough to have their say. Joseph may have found in them an echo of his own youthful enthusiasm and commitment, urging him to take the important step. Jacob did not need to be told why they were there; he was full of joy as Joseph hoped he would be. He sensed the importance of the visit. He may have been anxious about the future of these two lads of whom he had seen so little. He may have wondered if Joseph's faith still had the warmth and fervor that had bound them so closely in the old days.

We should not underestimate the significance of this visit, or what it meant in terms of personal heart-searching to Joseph, or its costliness to both himself and his two boys. According to Calvin, it meant that Joseph "regarded it a greater privilege to be a son of Jacob than to preside over a hundred kingdoms. . . . In bringing his sons with him he acted as if he would emancipate them from the country in which they had been born and restore them to their own stock. For they could not be reckoned among the progeny of Abraham without rendering themselves detested by the Egyptians." On Joseph's part it was also a fresh declaration to his father and to God of where his heart lay. He wanted to receive his father's deathbed blessing himself. The whole experience involved a recommitment of himself to the God of his fathers. It is Luther who points out that Joseph shines, once again, as an example to follow. The New Testament often warns us that after beginning with ardor and devotion and even maturing promisingly, we can fail in the long run. "By your endurance you will gain your souls," Jesus says to us (Luke 21:19 — "By standing firm you will gain life," NIV); and the endurance he is referring to here is the steady patience of a love that is always glowing with warm zeal.

Too often, as we become "wise," long-term servants of the Christian course within the church, we lose our warmth and zeal towards Christ himself, and we become unaware of the deep inward shift that has taken place. "I have this against you," said Jesus to certain prominent members of the church at Ephesus, "You have lost your early love" (Rev. 2:4, NEB). As our circumstances change and we pass through each further stage of life we need to examine ourselves, continually asking the question, Where is your heart? The question should perhaps be put to us more often by our preachers. We require a continual program of evangelism within the circle of church life itself — aimed at bringing those who are already professing Christians to personal recommitment.

Jacob — The Deathbed Blessing

Jacob sought, on his deathbed, to pass on to each of his children a formal "blessing" of a quite special nature, something he believed was a matter of duty. God had ordained that such a custom, possibly common elsewhere, should be solemnly observed within his special family circle as one generation moved into another at this stage in their early development as his people.

Jacob no doubt recalled the time in his own youth when he had received such "blessing" from his father Isaac, at the time when the old man thought himself about to die. Admittedly, the circumstances had been shameful, and yet God had inspired Isaac's utterance. Jacob's life from that very moment had begun to change. God had led him to Bethel (28:10-19) to experience there for the first time his personal presence and powerful assuring Word, and to know himself forgiven and accepted. Jacob must have expected that the Spirit of God would again come to be present and to inspire the spoken blessings he would now pass on to his sons and their descendants. We are told that in his weakness he "summoned his strength and sat up in bed" to be able to bless, yet he knew that his all-too-human speech was being powerfully taken over by God.

In giving such blessing the right hand was regarded as stronger than the left. Joseph had naturally placed the boys so that Manasseh, the older of the two, would be blessed by the right hand; Ephraim, in a secondary place, would be blessed by the left. Jacob felt himself inspired by God to cross his hands as he blessed the boys. He knew that in doing this he was canceling the priority established by birth order. He obviously believed that it was the will of the Spirit to cut across such natural rank.

Joseph was displeased. *"Not so, my father, for this one is the first-born; put your right hand upon his head"* (v. 18, RSV). It is strange that Joseph reverted to such strict legalism in this matter; though he himself had been nearly the youngest in his family, he had experienced great favor from God. Jacob pled with him simply to accept what God had done: Manasseh will not lack anything because of the special blessing on Ephraim. He too will be great, for God has inspired the blessing and his Word will not be in vain.

In passing, it is worth comparing what Jacob was hoping for as a result of his obedience, with what we who are pastors are seeking when we preach and at times administer the sacraments. If we are fully aware of the implications of our task, we too will be praying and expecting, as Jacob was, that God will be present to take over the words we utter, the ceremonies we fulfill, and indeed to some extent the elements we use; that God will make them meaningful and powerful in the lives of those who hear what we say and receive what we have to give. Thinking along these lines, we may also be justified in calling Jacob's deathbed blessing a "unique family sacrament."

"The Angel Who Has Redeemed Me from All Evil"

Jacob, uttering these words on his deathbed, must have regarded his life as a long story of deliverance from one evil after another. He could remember thankfully how time and again, through self-will and failure to trust and obey God he had drifted helplessly into troubles and dangers from which God in pure mercy had intervened to deliver him. There had been that first time when alone at Bethel (28:10-17) God had made himself real as his savior. There had been the time when the future of his whole family was threatened by the bitter and just anger of his uncle Laban, when the same gracious "God of Bethel" had again appeared at the crucial moment (31:11-29). There had been the miracle of his encounter with Esau on the way home from Paddan-aram, when his own life and the safety of his caravan had again come under threat, for Esau was bent on doing harm. The "angel" had come again, strangely interceding; there had been reconciliation instead of revenge (32:6–33:11). Then there had been the family apostasy — the secret worshiping of false gods — at the time when Simeon and Levi's folly had roused the deadly anger of the whole neighborhood. Again God had appeared at the right time, taken them back to Bethel and brought them all to a cleansing repentance (35:1-5). Then, with old age approaching, Jacob had finally and even more shamefully lapsed again, losing control of his family and his destiny, and it had happened again — the Lord's deliverance — this time with Joseph as the agent!

Note the final prominence, for old Jacob, of this figure of "the angel." Jacob could certainly talk and think of God in other ways when he wanted to express his faith. The family tradition and his own experience had taught him of God the creator who dwelt in heaven as ruler and "judge of all the earth" (Gen. 18:25), and who would surely always do what is right. Yet here and now before these two lads he spoke simply of "the angel." He can pray to the angel as he prays to God. His deepest question about who God is and what

God does seems to have been answered through his encounter with the angel. For Jacob, the angel was there together with God; the angel came from God, represented God, and was God. Jacob did not probe further into what seemed to be even then "worthy of full acceptance" (1 Tim. 1:15).

We have already read of this "angel of the Lord" caring for Hagar in her desolation (16:7-14) and calling to Abraham at a critical moment (22:11). Without realizing it, Abraham had entertained the angel of the Lord (10.1ff.; cf. Heb. 13:2). We will meet him again as he is sent in front of the wilderness tribes — to be their guide, to drive out their enemies, to speak with God's voice (Exod. 23:20-23; 32:34), and even to take God's place as a tolerable substitute when they could not bear to experience his naked presence (Exod. 33:2-3). Isaiah 63:9 (see NIV and KJV) can still be read as speaking of the "angel of his presence" who became the savior of Israel in distress.

We may link up all such passages with the repeated New Testament insistence that the Son of God — before he came in the flesh — not only took part in inspiring and directing the course of Old Testament history, but from time to time specially intervened in it, clothing himself temporarily in the form of an angel or even of a man and making his presence and his will known to chosen servants and prophets in ways that foreshadowed his incarnation. It was Jacob's privilege to be given familiarity with this heavenly visitor — the one who was "in the beginning with God" (John 1:2), who himself was God (v. 1), and who "became flesh and lived among us" (1:14).

One Generation to Another

When Jacob sat up in bed to bless those around him there was much more on his mind than performing a last sacramental rite. Everything we read here and in the following chapter may be seen as a sign of his deep concern to be continually faithful, on a much deeper level, in a matter of even greater importance. The two "blessings" he had poured out on Pharaoh during their short encounter were simply the spontaneous utterance of a heart and mind overflowing with gratitude for recent "blessed" experiences. Jacob was concerned, as long as he could muster the strength, to give his testimony to those who came after him of how good, forgiving, powerful, and faithful God had been to him. The psalmist had his like in mind: "One generation shall laud your works to another, and shall declare your mighty acts" (Ps. 145:4). In the latter years of Jacob's life he had been shamefully conscious of how often and how much he had failed in the task, but God had brought him back. The story of his failure and restoration will now enrich his testimony. And now he discovers again that even in his weakness, and perhaps because of it, as he seeks to serve God with all his heart and soul and strength the words he speaks ring with reality. He believes his family will remember and talk about the praise of God, the stories of his grace and goodness, the exhortations and warnings he has tried to pass on. He hopes that in recalling his testimony they will hear a word that will enter their history and profoundly affect what happens to them. He believes that in their whole tradition, in their way of life and their attitudes, they will be challenged and helped by the personal influence, the teaching about God and life, the stories of encounters with God and of the works of God, that he, under divine inspiration, has handed on. And as a result, a name they will give to their God in years to come will be "the mighty God of Jacob."

Paul's word to Timothy, "Guard what has been entrusted to you" (1 Tim. 6:20), is a cogent reminder that even now we have much in our church life (and indeed also in what we can still regard as a good and healthy, even "Christian" tradition) that is worth treasuring. We are meant to "guard" it so that it can be passed on to those who follow us. Each generation has more to hand down to history than great church buildings, creeds, confessions, printed Bibles, well-organized charities, missions, and caring institutions. Long after we ourselves are gone our prayers can count, and our example can be remembered. Our approach to life, our words and thoughts, our attitude to evil, to worship and the Bible, can by God's grace become an influence that helps turn the mind and life of others towards God. Of course what we each as individuals can give to the future will seem only a small current in the mighty flow of the world's life, affecting only a very small sphere. But not one sparrow falling to the ground is insignificant to God. Not one place in the universe is beyond his concern, or beyond the working of his gracious power.

CHAPTER 12

Prophetic Oracles on the Twelve Tribes

Genesis 49:1-28

49 Then Jacob called his sons, and said: "Gather around, that I may tell you what will happen to you in days to come.

² Assemble and hear, O sons of Jacob;
    listen to Israel your father.

³ Reuben, you are my first-born,
    my might and the first fruits of my vigor,
    excelling in rank and excelling in power.
⁴ Unstable as water, you shall no longer excel
    because you went up to your father's bed;
    thus you defiled it — you went up onto my couch!

⁵ Simeon and Levi are brothers;
    weapons of violence are their swords.
⁶ May I never come into their council;
    may I not be joined to their company –
for in their anger they killed men,
    and at their whim they hamstrung oxen.
⁷ Cursed be their anger, for it is fierce,
    and their wrath, for it is cruel!

I will divide them in Jacob,
    and scatter them in Israel.

8 Judah, your brothers shall praise you,
    your hand shall be on the neck of your enemies;
    your father's sons shall bow down before you.
9 Judah is a lion's whelp;
    from the prey, my son, you have gone up
    He crouches down, he stretches out like a lion,
    like a lioness — who dares rouse him up?
10 The scepter shall not depart from Judah,
    nor the ruler's staff from between his feet,
    until tribute comes to him;
    and the obedience of the peoples is his.
11 Binding his foal to the vine,
    and his donkey's colt to the choice vine,
    he washes his garments in wine,
    and his robe in the blood of grapes;
12 his eyes are darker than wine,
    and his teeth whiter than milk.

13 Zebulun shall settle at the shore of the sea;
    he shall be a haven for ships,
    and his border shall be at Sidon.

14 Issachar is a strong donkey,
    lying down between the sheepfolds;
15 he saw that a resting place was good,
    and that the land was pleasant;
    so he bowed his shoulder to the burden,
    and became a slave at forced labor.

16 Dan shall judge his people,
    as one of the tribes of Israel.
17 Dan shall be a snake by the roadside,

a viper along the path,
 that bites the horse's heels,
  so that its rider falls backward.

18 I wait for your salvation, O Lord.

19 Gad shall be raided by raiders,
 but he shall raid at their heels.

20 Asher's food shall be rich,
 and he shall provide royal delicacies.

21 Naphtali is a doe let loose,
 that bears lovely fawns.

22 Joseph is a fruitful bough,
 a fruitful bough by a spring;
 his branches run over the wall.
23 The archers fiercely attacked him;
 they shot at him and pressed him hard.
24 Yet his bow remained taut,
 and his arms were made agile
by the hands of the Mighty One of Jacob,
 by the name of the Shepherd, the Rock of Israel,
25 by the God of your father, who will help you,
 by the Almighty who will bless you,
 with blessings of heaven above,
blessings of the deep that lies beneath,
 blessings of the breasts and of the womb.
26 The blessings of your father
 are stronger than the blessings of the eternal mountains,
 the bounties of the everlasting hills;
may they be on the head of Joseph,
 on the brow of him who was set apart from his brothers.

²⁷ Benjamin is a ravenous wolf,
>   in the morning devouring the prey,
>   and at evening dividing the spoil."

²⁸ All these are the twelve tribes of Israel, and this is what their father said to them when he blessed them, blessing each one of them with a suitable blessing.

Introduction

Jacob in this chapter addresses a series of oracles, one to each of his children, telling them prophetically the kind of future that is about to open up to them. At the close of the chapter we are told that as he spoke these prophecies, Jacob also *"blessed each of them with a suitable blessing"* (v. 28). In the oracles as we now have them, addressed to the various tribes, there is no record of the actual blessing, and we have to assume that whoever compiled this chapter found in these blessings nothing significant enough to preserve.

The first three oracles Jacob uttered as he sought to bless are words of censure and warning (vv. 3-7). He must have been aware that each of these tribes, at the time he spoke, had strangely reacted against Joseph's recall to the service of God, and were entrenching themselves in attitudes and ways that made it impossible to receive the blessing Jacob longed to give. He therefore has to warn them, in fatherly love and hope, that if they persist they will come under judgment and be broken. God is "not dragging them back as guilty fugitives to judgment," says Calvin, "he is acting as a physician rather than a judge, who refuses to spare because he wants to heal."

Those who tend to be critical of the biblical text will undoubtedly have difficulties with this one. Many of these poems imply such accurate knowledge of a tribe's future area of settlement, and of later conditions generally, that those who exclude the possibility of detailed predictive prophecy regard this chapter as a later collection of oracles inserted here by a final editor because this section of the book of Genesis seemed a suitable context for it. But it would be a pity if doubts about the authenticity or accuracy of the words obscure the essential witness they are here to give.

Oracles of Censure

Reuben (cf. Gen. 35:22) has been a rather weak and foolish man, but privileged by being firstborn in the family. His status has made him excel in arrogance when his defects should have made him humble. His eminence within the family has made him feel secure, and he has failed to curb his fatal passions. The word of God to him through Jacob is a word of warning to all gifted and privileged people born with great potential but lacking self-control:

> Pre-eminent in pride, pre-eminent in power,
> Unstable as water, you shall not have pre-eminence.
>
> (vv. 3-4, RSV)

Reuben's successors in the tribe that took his name seem to have ignored Jacob's warning, and the implied threat behind the word to Reuben was fulfilled. There is no mention of any leader of Israel arising at any time from among the Reubenites, and later mention of them seems to indicate that as a community they were of little service to the people of God.

Jacob feared that the violent cruelty of Simeon and Levi, which they had justified in the name of God, had itself arisen out of a deep mindset that might remain unaltered by the passing of time. There was real danger that this trait would prevail among their posterity, giving rise to false ways of talking and thinking, and to brutal ways of dealing with other people. Cursed are those who allow their policies to be dictated by anger! (49:7). God will surely scatter the peoples who delight in war! (Ps. 68:30). The opening words of the oracle to Simeon and Levi are to be read as much more than a trite statement of family relationship. Jacob is warning those around him of the camaraderie that emboldens people to use their weapons for violent purposes:

> Simeon and Levi are brothers;
>> weapons of violence are their swords.

(v. 5)

The fact that both brothers gave good religious reasons for their awful deed at Shechem fills the old man's soul with horror. No one must even approach the company of such men, or lend an ear for one moment to talk that can justify such ruthlessness:

> O my soul, come not into their counsel;
>> O my spirit, be not be joined to their company.

(v. 6, RSV)

The oracle prophesies the breakup of both Simeon and Levi as tribes. To prevent the danger of the renewal of their false brotherhood they were to be scattered and dispersed (cf. v. 7, NEB). The tribe of Simeon seems to have allowed itself to become absorbed in its dispersion.

The sons of Levi, though scattered, made good and became an instrument in the working out of God's purposes (cf. Josh. 21; Rev. 3:19, "Those whom I love, I reprove and chasten"). It was only in the case of Levi and his successors that these prophetic warnings proved fruitful. The tribe of Levi, denied a homeland of their own, accepted their punishment as given out of love. They repented, and proved it by their outstanding loyalty to Moses during the crisis of the Golden Calf (Exod. 32:25-28). As a reward and a sign of reacceptance they were appointed as priestly substitutes for the firstborn of all the other tribes; they were ordained to have the privilege in Israel "to do service in the tent of meeting" (Num. 8:15) and to carry the ark of the covenant — a truly important function in Israel's early history. Jacob's frank severity proved to have its wisdom. We are reminded time and again in the New Testament that as we speak together about Christ and his love we must not fail to be as frank with our warnings (2 Tim. 4:2) as we are earnest and passionate in our appeals and invitations.

The Lion of Judah

Judah, your brothers shall praise you;
    your hand shall be on the neck of your enemies;
your father's sons shall bow down before you.

                                          (v. 8)

Judah is to be given the leadership that his three brothers have forfeited. The posterity of Judah will produce a dynasty of leaders who will be kings wielding the "scepter" and the "ruler's staff," the insignia of royalty. In the years to come (cf. 49:1) in succession of this dynasty a king will appear to whom all peoples shall give obedience (v. 10). In this verse we have the clearest reference, since the story of Abraham began, to the fact that the people of God are destined to produce for themselves and the whole world a Messiah. A hint is also given here that when this one appears there will also dawn on the earth a new Messianic age. We are given a picture of this king:

Binding his foal to the vine
    and his ass's colt to the choice vine

121

> he washes his garment in wine
>   and his vesture in the blood of grapes.

(v. 11, RSV)

The language suggests a time of prodigious fertility, indeed a renewed earth. Life under this king will be lived in a land of peace and plenty. Vines will be so plentiful and luxuriant that wine can be used for water, and fruitful branches can be used as tethering posts for animals.

Descriptions of this Messiah and of the Messianic age occur frequently in other books of the Old Testament. David was eventually born, of the tribe of Judah, and all Israel came and chose him as ruler of their nation (2 Sam. 5:1-3). Nathan the prophet then promised that a successor to this throne, one of David's lineage, would eventually enjoy rule over a kingdom "established forever" (2 Sam. 7:2ff.). Later prophets spoke often of a coming Messiah arising from the tribe of Judah, from the same root that had produced David (cf., e.g., Mic. 5:1-5; Amos 9:11-15; Isa. 9:6ff., 11:1ff.; Jer. 23:5-8). They associated his reign with an age in which the whole earth would be renewed, and the nations would live together in peace and prosperity (Isa. 11:6ff.; Joel 3:18; Zech. 8:9; Mic. 4:1ff.).

In the book of Revelation there is an unforgettable picture of a strange event in heaven. The throne of God is visible, and at the right hand of it a scroll is seen with seven seals. Only as these seals are broken can the history of this world be allowed to move on towards its climax. Only as the book is opened can this history with all its riddles be understood. There is tension and sorrow in heaven because no one can be found worthy or able to open the scroll or look into it. Suddenly there appears in heaven one who is worthy to take this scroll and open it. As he takes the book to begin his task, he appears as "a lamb standing as though it had been slain," but it is explained to the seer of the vision that he is "the lion of the tribe of Judah, the root of David who has conquered so

122

that he can open the scroll and its seven seals" (Rev. 5:1-5). By these words we are referred again this very old prophecy, attributed to Jacob, of Judah as the conquering lion (v. 9). But in the same shimmering image we are given to understand that the Messiah has indeed come, the one to whom belongs all power and obedience (v. 10).

Each in His Place with His Gift

Judah may provide the ruler. But each tribe is meant to have its place and special function in the community that is to be under such leadership. Jacob's poem is down to earth in its details, telling how each of the tribes will contribute to the welfare of the future Israel. Gad and Dan, for instance, will be buffer states. They will take the shock of encounters with raiding and invading armies. The men of Gad will raid back in self-defense (49:19); the men of Dan will harass the great invading armies that cross their territory (v. 17). The tribe of Dan will also give an example to the others in its administration of justice (v. 16).

The poem expresses admiration for the enterprise of the tribe of Zebulun in populating the coastlands and developing seamanship and shipping, so important to the trade and wealth of a nation. Elsewhere Zebulun is accorded praise for its single-minded valor in the defense of Israel (1 Chron. 12:33). Asher is commended for a contribution of a different nature: producing luxuries for the table ("dishes fit for a king," NEB). The reference to Naphtali as a "doe let loose that bears lovely fawns" (v. 21; cf. NEB: *"a spreading terebinth putting forth lovely boughs"*) seems to indicate that this tribe's talents will add graceful and delicate touches to the life of God's people. Though Issachar is also praised elsewhere for the wisdom of its counsel and valor in the nation's defense (cf. 1 Chron. 12:32), the enigmatic words of Jacob's oracle are sometimes interpreted as a reproach. Its people were endowed with great powers of endurance. If they had lived within the area allotted to them, they would have greatly enriched the life of the nation. But there opens up for them the chance of easy money by providing immigrant labor to a neighboring people. For the sake of ease and security they accept the humiliation of servile occupation under alien masters:

> Issachar is a strong ass,
>> crouching between the sheepfolds;
> he saw that a resting place was good,
>> and that the land was pleasant.
> So he bowed his shoulder to bear,
>> and became a slave at forced labor.
>
> (vv. 14-15, RSV)

The last oracle was about the tribe of Benjamin. It sounds, on a first reading, as if it were a warning against self-centered greed:

> Benjamin is a ravenous wolf,
>> in the morning devouring the prey,
> and at evening dividing the spoil.
>
> (v. 27)

Commentators point out, however, that elsewhere in Holy Scripture this tribe is praised (cf. Deut. 33:12) and that its men were valiant in their defense of the community (cf. Judges 20:21). When Luther interpreted the oracle he remembered that the apostle Paul was "of the tribe of Benjamin" (cf. Phil. 3:5), and applied the saying to Paul's career. "He first devoured the holy Stephen like a wolf, and spent the rest of his days sharing the Gospel with the whole world."

Joseph

Though he is not destined to be the forefather of the anointed leader of the people of God, a glorious and fruitful future seems to be outlined here for Joseph's posterity. They will keep in touch with God no matter how harsh their lot or how severe their suffering under persecution and attack, for Joseph himself had been made strong and immovable *"by the hands of the Mighty One of Jacob, by the name of the Shepherd, the Rock of Israel"* (v. 24). There is no hint here of what was actually to happen — of the split between Judah in the south and the confederation of northern tribes under the dominant influence of Joseph's descendents. As far as recorded history is concerned, we know that things finally went wrong with the tribe of Ephraim and indeed with the other nine northern tribes who were dominated by its influence. God certainly lavished his care upon them and pled with them to return to him and avoid their self-destruction. Great prophets like Elijah, Elisha, Hosea, and Amos worked, preached, and prayed in the struggle to save them from idolatry and Baal worship and from their social injustices. In the end the kingdom was destroyed. The people were deported by the Assyrians to the north, to be enslaved, and they seemed to disappear entirely from the stage of human history.

Generations later, the prophet Jeremiah, working in Jerusalem, saw to his own horror that the people of Judah were even more idolatrous, sexually immoral, unjust and corrupt in their politics, than these northern tribes had been. If God was going to save the people of Judah, he could not cast off the tribes of Ephraim and the others associated with it! Jeremiah could not accept that the last word about Joseph's descendents should be so contrary to the hopes and prayers of Jacob and Rachel. Alluding to the place where Rachel was buried, he wrote the following words:

Thus says the Lord:
"A voice is heard in Ramah,

lamentation and bitter weeping.
Rachel is weeping for her children;
She refuses to be comforted for her children,
    because they are no more."

(Jer. 31:15)

Early in his ministry Jeremiah felt inspired to utter oracles pleading with these lost tribes, and especially with Ephraim, to return to
God, in his imagination he seemed to hear them returning with a song
of repentance on their lips (cf. Jer. 3:11f., 21f.). Later, when he tried to
describe the time when the Kingdom of God will finally come, he was
comforted by a word of assurance from God that the children of Joseph, the cherished child of Jacob and Rachel, are still dear to God too.

Is Ephraim my dear son?
    Is he the child I delight in?
As often as I speak against him
    I still remember him.
Therefore I am deeply moved for him
    I will surely have mercy on him, says the Lord.

(Jer. 31:20)

Jeremiah's belief in this future, his confident Word about these
tribes in the face of what must have seemed an irreversible verdict of
history, is one of the greatest affirmations of faith in the Old Testament. His laments over what are sometimes called the "lost ten tribes"
have been linked speculatively with other Old Testament texts. What
might have happened to them? Did they come back to God among the
God-fearing gentiles who figured so strongly in the spread of the early
church? Or can they be located today among the nations and tribes of
the earth? The futility of such speculation should remind us not to interpret the Old Testament too dogmatically. We believe these texts
bear witness to the everlasting love of God, and to the promises fulfilled in Jesus Christ himself. We needn't ask more of them.

126

CHAPTER 13

The Waiting Israel

Genesis 49:29–50:26

49 ²⁹ Then he charged them, saying to them, "I am about to be gathered to my people. Bury me with my ancestors — in the cave in the field of Ephron the Hittite, ³⁰ in the cave in the field at Machpelah, near Mamre, in the land of Canaan, in the field that Abraham bought from Ephron the Hittite as a burial site. ³¹ There Abraham and his wife Sarah were buried; there Isaac and his wife Rebekah were buried; and there I buried Leah — ³² the field and the cave that is in it were purchased from the Hittites." When Jacob ended his charge to his sons, he drew up his feet into the bed, breathed his last, and was gathered to his people.

50 Then Joseph threw himself on his father's face and wept over him and kissed him. ² Joseph commanded the physicians in his service to embalm his father. So the physicians embalmed Israel; ³ they spent forty days in doing this, for that is the time required for embalming. And the Egyptians wept for him seventy days.

⁴ When the days of weeping for him were past, Joseph addressed the household of Pharaoh, "If now I have found favor with you, please speak to Pharaoh as follows: ⁵ My father made me swear an oath; he said, 'I am about to die. In the tomb that I hewed out for myself in the land of Canaan, there you shall bury me.' Now therefore let me go up,

so that I may bury my father; then I will return." 6Pharaoh answered, "Go up, and bury your father, as he made you swear to do."

7 So Joseph went up to bury his father. With him went up all the servants of Pharaoh, the elders of his household, and all the elders of the land of Egypt, 8 as well as all the household of Joseph, his brothers, and his father's household. Only their children, their flocks, and their herds were left in the land of Goshen. 9 Both chariots and charioteers went up with him. It was a very great company. 10 When they came to the threshing floor of Atad, which is beyond the Jordan, they held there a very great and sorrowful lamentation; and observed a time of mourning for his father seven days. 11 When the Canaanite inhabitants of the land saw the mourning on the threshing floor of Atad, they said, "This is a grievous mourning on the part of the Egyptians." Therefore the place was named Abel-mizraim; it is beyond the Jordan. 12 Thus his sons did for him as he had instructed them. 13 They carried him to the land of Canaan and buried him in the cave of the field at Machpelah, the field near Mamre, which Abraham bought as a burial site from Ephron the Hittite. 14 After he had buried his father, Joseph returned to Egypt with his brothers and all who had gone up with him to bury his father.

15 Realizing that their father was dead, Joseph's brothers said, "What if Joseph still bears a grudge against us and pays us back in full for all the wrong that we did to him?" 16 So they approached Joseph, saying, "Your father gave this instruction before he died, 17 'Say to Joseph: I beg you, forgive the crime of your brothers and the wrong they did in harming you.' Now therefore please forgive the crime of the servants of the God of your father." Joseph wept when they spoke to him. 18 Then his brothers also wept, fell down before him, and said, "We are here as your slaves." 19 But Joseph said to them, "Do not be afraid! Am I in the place of God? 20 Even though you intended to do harm to me, God intended it for good, in order to preserve a numerous people, as he is doing today. 21 So have no fear; I myself will provide for you and your little ones." In this way he reassured them, speaking kindly to them.

22 So Joseph remained in Egypt, he and his father's household; and Joseph lived one hundred ten years. 23 Joseph saw Ephraim's children of the third generation; the children of Machir son of Manasseh were also born on Joseph's knees.

24 Then Joseph said to his brothers, "I am about to die; but God will surely come to you, and bring you up out of this land to the land that he swore to Abraham, to Isaac, and to Jacob." 25 So Joseph made the Israelites swear, saying, "When God comes to you, you shall carry up my bones from here." 26 And Joseph died, being one hundred ten years old; he was embalmed and placed in a coffin in Egypt.

The Burial

When Jacob died, he spoke of himself as about to be *"gathered to my people"* (v. 29). He wished to be buried *"in the cave in the field at Machpelah"* (v. 30), the place that Abraham's body had lain along with that of Sarah, Isaac, Rebekah, and Leah. Yet the phrase *"gathered to my people"* seems to mean more than simply having one's body buried in the same grave as one's ancestors. There is no reason why God should not have given the Patriarchs some anticipation of the good things to come. The author of the Epistle to the Hebrews was convinced that Abraham, who sojourned all his days in Canaan, looked forward to a "better country," to the "city which has foundations whose builder and maker is God" (Heb. 11:9, 10, 16). The Patriarchs, he claimed, "all died in faith, not having received what was promised, but having seen it and greeted it from afar" (Heb. 11:13).

It was natural that as Jacob approached his time of death he should ask that his body be taken back to Canaan for burial, and request an oath from Joseph that finally he would lie with his fathers in the land God had promised them. The burial place, a cave in the field at Machpelah — the first piece of land owned by him on behalf of his family — had been bought by Abraham from the sons of Heth. Its purchase was taken as a pledge from God that one day the whole land would belong to his successors.

The pomp associated with his burial was uncharacteristic of Jacob. But it was Egyptian practice, and when Joseph sought permission from Pharaoh to go and bury his father he possibly had to suffer the embarrassment of allowing his host country a free expression of its regard for his family. He may have felt he could accept their generous tribute as a token of their respect for his father's faith. Dr. Derek Kidner suggests that the united journey of the Egyptians and Israelites to Canaan can be taken by us as a sign in miniature of the final fulfillment of one of Isaiah's prophecies of the future of Israel: "I am coming to gather all the nations as an offering to the Lord, upon horses, and in chariots, and in litters, and upon mules, and upon dromedaries, to my holy mountain, Jerusalem" (Isa. 66:18ff.).

"Am I in the Place of God?"

The loss of Jacob had an immediate and devastating effect on the morale of Joseph's brothers. When they saw that their father was dead, they said, *"It may be that Joseph will hate us, and pay us back for all the evil which we did to him"* (v. 15, RSV). So real and intense was their fear that they sent a messenger to ask Joseph to spare their lives, and they claimed that Jacob himself before his death had urged them to plead in this way for forgiveness (vv. 16-17). We can understand the brothers. They were just like most of us, and this was one of their bad moments. In strange surroundings, they had suddenly lost the security of the old family environment. They had been entirely dependent, in going to Egypt, on their father's decision, and they had grown more and more to depend on his leadership and wisdom — and now he was gone!

Joseph *"reassured them and comforted them"* (v. 21, RSV). He may have blamed himself for being too aloof in recent years, and for being too busy to notice and understand the strain they had lived under in Egypt. They were as sheep without a shepherd, and he was moved with compassion (Matt. 9:36). They needed some kind of leadership within the family to replace that of Jacob. They seem to have expected this of Joseph at this time, and their visit to him was a kind of invitation to assume the responsibility. Judah, as we have seen, had played a significant part in the family, but while they were in Egypt it was clear that no one deserved priority over Joseph. The younger brother quietly stepped into Jacob's place. *"Am I in the place of God?"* he asked. It was an acutely challenging pastoral question.

He laid his finger exactly on what had gone wrong with them. As they had settled down in Egypt they had come to depend so unquestioningly on Jacob's leadership that he had taken the place of God in their lives, and now that Jacob had gone they were turning to Joseph. His words were a reproach. They had failed to keep fresh in their minds and hearts the redeeming grace that had so wonderfully transformed their family life; their world of faith had become so small that they were clinging to mere human personality and leadership!

Joseph pled with them to lift up their hearts again to the Lord, and reminded them again of the full dimension of God's power and love. He repeated what he had said to them those seventeen years earlier: *"Do not be afraid! . . . Even though you intended to do harm to me, God intended it for good, in order to preserve a numerous people, as he is doing today. So have no fear"* (vv. 19-21). Surely now, they could see it more clearly than ever — for the proof was there before them! They were still in the hands of the God of their fathers, who was continuing to work all things together for good to those who loved and trusted him. God had obviously declared his forgiveness by a deed of salvation that only sheer perverseness could deny! God remained now as ever the powerful and faithful one who had proved himself again

131

and again to Abraham and the fathers — the one who sees, provides, controls, and guides — the mighty God of Jacob!

Only the pure in heart can see God (Matt. 5:8). The pure in heart are those who allow God his supreme place within. Joseph's searching question to his brothers applies itself directly to many of us in our modern situation too. We often lack courage and assurance in the face of life's difficulties because we have no clear vision of God's love and power. This is because we, too, do not allow God the central place in our devotion. We prefer to keep him at a comfortable distance, in an allotted place that does not upset our established way of life. We do not wish him to replace all the ideas and substitutes for God that have so far ruled our self-arranged life. We are like the children of Israel in the wilderness. When God came near to speak to them they were terrified, and they repelled his further advance. They pled with Moses to be God's stand-in. "You speak to us," they said, "and we will hear; but let not God speak to us, lest we die" (Exod. 20:19; cf. Deut. 5:25ff.).

As Joseph pointed to God he tried to efface himself. He reminds us of John the Baptist disclaiming his own importance as he pointed to Jesus. "He must increase but I must decrease" (John 3:30). He himself tried to be nothing but "a voice" (1:23). Those of us who are pastors are ourselves too prone to get in the way. God trusts us with ministry to others in his name, and as we fulfill this ministry he indeed allows us at times even to stand "in his place" (see pp. 45, 110) to speak his word, to offer the help he inspires, to share the good he gives — but only in his name, only as witnesses pointing away from ourselves to him. Too often we fail even to try to hide ourselves, and our right hand is too conscious of what our left hand is doing.

How are the trustful and seeking people around us going to be most surely helped by our ministry and counsel to enter the glorious liberty of the children of God? Joseph was trying his best to say what later leaders of his people would say more adroitly. The great prophets spoke of one who dwells "in the high and holy place and also with

132

him who is of a contrite and humble spirit, to revive the spirit of the humble and to revive the heart of the contrite" (Isa. 57:15). They spoke not only of how he overrules transgressions by making evil work for good, but also of how he sweeps away our sins like a dissolving mist (Isa. 44:22), and of how he will finally cast them all into the depths of the sea (Mic. 7:19). Today we can not only use the prophets' richer language, we can also speak of Jesus Christ, the one who "carried our sins to the gibbet" (1 Pet. 2:24, NEB), thus disposing of them forever. Far more effectively than a Joseph, Christ himself can dethrone all false substitutes. He alone can stand safely in the place of God, because he has the eternal right to do so.

"God Will Come to You"

The writer of the New Testament letter to the Hebrews regards Joseph's last recorded words as important: "By faith, Joseph, at the end of his life made mention of the exodus of the Israelites and gave directions concerning his bones" (Heb. 11:22). In the incident referred to, *"Joseph said to his brothers, 'I am about to die; but God will surely come to you, and bring you up out of this land to the land that he swore to Abraham, to Isaac, and to Jacob.' So Joseph made the Israelites swear, saying, "When God comes to you, you shall carry my bones up from here'"* (vv. 24-25). Joseph was repeating what God said clearly to Jacob at Beersheba before the migration to Egypt. He did not explain how the promise would be fulfilled. The outline of the future was vague though the promise was sure. Joseph repeated it twice: *"God will come to you."* He did not say whether it would happen soon or later.

This long period into which they were now entering would be a time of silent waiting until they came under fierce oppression by a Pharaoh who did not know Joseph (Exod. 1:8), and Moses appeared to rescue them. We have no ground for assuming that any arresting or important Word came to them during this long period. If there had been any such prophetic oracle or vision it surely would have found a place in the tradition, alongside the stories of the Patriarchs and their teaching. But there is no such reference anywhere in Holy Scripture. We cannot help comparing Israel's life in Egypt after the Patriarchal age to that of the waiting years after the age of the great prophets. For many generations the voice of prophecy ceased. Yet Israel did not die. The people had their holy scrolls, their cultus, their synagogues, and their teachers, and God used these things in a powerful way to sustain their life. They had enough to live on triumphantly, to keep them faithful and to rouse their expectancy of the coming new age — so that people like Simeon and Anna, like Mary and Joseph and Elizabeth, were there to greet it.

Similarly, from the death of Joseph till the coming of Moses, the children of Israel had to nurture their life, sharpen their minds, and find their inspiration within the tradition handed down to them by the Patriarchs. Yet they had much to go on and to live by. They knew about altars and sacrifices, about sacred meals and blessings. They knew how to meet God in quiet ways in worship. They found the stories and the repetition of God's Word to their fathers a living source for themselves. Moreover they had leaders and teachers to replace Joseph and Jacob. We have to remember that when Moses was sent back to them after his vision of God he was told that he would find Aaron coming out to meet him — Aaron his brother whom God had also been quietly preparing. We read of how Moses and Aaron gathered all the elders of the people, of how Aaron spoke to them, and of how when they "heard that the Lord had visited the people of Israel and that he had seen their affliction, they bowed their heads and worshipped" (Exod. 4:27-31). It was the day they had been waiting for, for generations — the fulfillment of the promise: *"God will come to you."*

In his last request to his family to keep his body in their own possession, and to carry back his bones with them when they left Egypt (v. 25), Joseph once again proved himself wise and true. The Egyptians no doubt were prepared to give him an honored place among their own dead. As we all know, it was their custom to put people like him — people with wealth and possessions — in a massive tomb to be sealed and preserved for some kind of afterlife. Joseph allowed them to embalm his body, but it was to be placed in a coffin and kept among his own people. Though he was dead, the presence of his very bones would remind his brothers and descendants of what God had done for him and through him, and of the promise of the land, and of the blessing.